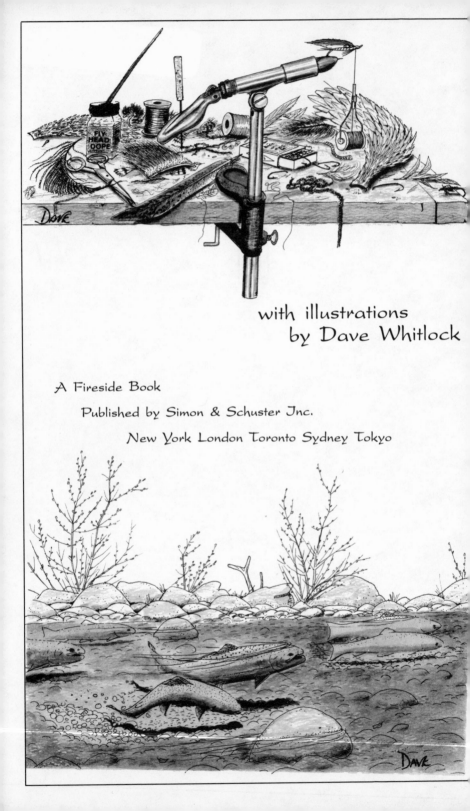

with illustrations
by Dave Whitlock

A Fireside Book

Published by Simon & Schuster Inc.

New York London Toronto Sydney Tokyo

# The Year
## of the Angler

### Steve Raymond

First Fireside Edition, 1988
Published by Simon & Schuster Inc.
Simon & Schuster Building
Rockefeller Center
1230 Avenue of the Americas
New York, New York 10020
Published by arrangement with Winchester Press
FIRESIDE and colophon are registered trademarks
of Simon & Schuster Inc.

Designed by Kikkon Designs
Manufactured in the United States of America

10 9 8 7 6 5 4 3 2    Pbk.

Library of Congress Cataloging in Publication Data
Raymond, Steve.
    The year of the angler.

    "A Fireside Book."
    1. Fly fishing.   2. Fishing—Northwest, Pacific.
I. Title.
SH456.R39   1988b      799.1'755      88-6538
ISBN 0-671-66174-4 Pbk.

*To Joan, Stephanie and Randy*
*—for sharing all the seasons*

# Contents

# Preface

Enos Bradner, Roderick Haig-Brown, Ben Hur Lampman . . . so begins the roll-call of Legend, as the subject of Western fishing comes up, which it does more and more often. It does because the preponderance of American quality angling has been moving steadily westward for now very nearly half a century. The great days of the storied Eastern streams had peaked by 1925, and by midcentury mid-Pennsylvania had become the last Eastern redoubt of the kind of fishing from which Legend is engendered. There on the rivers that served as the nearest American equivalent of those chalk streams that bracket the English Channel from Hampshire and from Normandy, the mantle of glory-cloudstuff that had earlier enveloped Gordon, Hewitt and La Branche began to weave itself around the figures of Fox, Grove and Marinaro, the masters of the minutiae, and even the prodigiously gifted young Schwiebert, who had come among them, precocious as a grilse invading the redds of spawning salmon, so far ahead of his normally allotted season.

History, with its peculiar propensity for repeating itself, now appears to be restaging the same play of Legend for the West Coast, complete even down to this latter detail of the casting, for we clearly discern, right beside the three venerable figures first mentioned, a fourth who is a much younger man but already stands tall among them.

Bradner, after all, is in his eighties, like Charlie Ritz, and even among such longevity-prone people as anglers, that has to be regarded as an obvious length of tooth; and as far back as 1965, when *A Leaf from French Eddy* first appeared, Lampman was already enshrined in a memorial edition; and as for the peerless Haig-Brown, he has retired, after many a long year, from the magistrate's bench, and as everyone knows, judges constitute a separate category of those who practically have to be born old; and now front and center in such company appears Steve Raymond, who is by contrast a mere stripling. It's only a couple of years ago that he took over the editorial reins of *The Flyfisher*, the official journal of the Federation of Fly Fishermen, and that virtually at the moment of the publication of *Kamloops*, his first book.

But he came on the scene full-armed, like Minerva from the brain of Jove, and not Methuselah himself could have found the time to do a more exhaustive job than he did in that brilliant book on the one unique fish, the Kamloops trout. All it left some of us asking was what could he possibly do for an encore? Well, we needn't have wasted any time wondering. Here, in *The Year of the Angler*, we have the answer, and it's stunning. This book is as clearly in a class by itself as its predecessor, yet the contrast between two books couldn't be more complete. Where that one stuck with single-minded and even dogged devotion to every possible ramification of only one subject, this one ranges over a veritable smorgasbord of subject matter, with a diversity of topic and treatment that would be bewildering in its variety if it were not endowed with homogeneity by the strict discipline of its yearbook form. It is a rich compound of nature-study, philosophy, history, ecology and environmental activism, demographics and social studies, aphorism and anecdote and—no I'm not going to shy away from this one—sheer poetry. The fishing encompasses both summer and winter steelhead, both Pacific and Atlantic salmon—the former in a busy industrial district and the latter in a lake formerly known as Mud!—and both kinds of trout fishing, seagoing and, I nearly said, sedentary (which of course the nonmigratory variety, at least as practiced here, is anything but), and there's even one excursion into cutthroat fishing by electronic tracking. Also thrown in at no apparent extra charge is a full-fledged mystery story, as well as the best trip to the Firehole that I for one have as yet encountered in print. What an angling menu!—and all within the Western region. It's enough to account for the greening of anglers' faces from some three-quarters to seven-eighths of the rest of America.

After reading *Kamloops* and now after reading this I can only echo the sporting poet John Gay in a thought he expressed for his own epitaph. The way he put it was:

> *Life is a jest, and all things show it.*
> *I thought so once, and now I know it.*

That's how I felt, then and now, about the promise and the performance of Steve Raymond, as an angling author.

—ARNOLD GINGRICH

# Foreword

The reader may notice that Arnold Gingrich never used the word "classic" in his Preface to the original 1973 edition of this book. With all the praise that he lavished upon both author and book, it certainly would have been easy to use that word. He refused to do so because he felt that no one man should label a book a classic; by his definition, a book could qualify as a classic only after years of appreciation.

Now, more than ten years after the original edition appeared, *The Year of the Angler* is being republished because it has been appreciated by a diverse fly-fishing audience. This is one of those rare books not bound by place or time. Anglers everywhere will share the thoughts and feelings expressed in these essays and stories of Northwestern fly fishing. If in truth it takes more than one generation to judge a book a classic then this reprint represents a giant step for *The Year of the Angler*.

There were compelling reasons for bringing this book back into print. It became evident that many fly fishermen wanted a copy of *The Year of the Angler* for their libraries. Antiquarian booksellers reported a brisk trade for used copies of the first edition at escalating prices.

The book's reputation was established immediately by the many fine reviews. The honors it received guaranteed that the reputation would grow through the years. It won the Governor's Award at the Washington State Festival of the Arts, and it was chosen by the American Booksellers Association as one of the select list of books presented to the President of the United States for the White House library.

Steve Raymond, of course, continued writing after the appearance of *The Year of the Angler*. He has contributed chapters to almost every estimable fly-fishing anthology published since 1973 (including *Fishing Moments of Truth, The Masters on the Dry Fly, The Masters on the Nymph, Stillwater Trout,* and *Waters Swift and Still*). His magazine articles, especially a series of short, insightful pieces in *Sports Illustrated,* have won him new devotees and satisfied old ones. The publication in 1980 of a revised edition of his first book, *Kamloops* (1971), verified both the worth of that well-researched work and the lasting popularity of the author.

A demand for *The Year of the Angler* made this new edition possible; the unique quality of the book made it necessary. All other fly-fishing books before or since have never quite filled the same niche in our literature, because Steve Raymond shared with the reader a view of an uncommon world—his own. By revealing something of himself in his stories, he colored each of them with his own feelings.

What makes *The Year of the Angler* such an excellent book? It is beautifully written, thoughtful, and at the same time entertaining. It is not a collection of rollicking humor, although there are moments of piercing wit. Overall, there is a gentle mixture of hope (chiefly with the discoveries of new waters) and despair (chiefly with the loss of favorite fisheries); by the end of the book, the feelings of melancholy balance with the joy. *The Year of the Angler* is an admirable fishing book because it is about more than fishing.

As William Humphrey cogently observed in *My Moby Dick*, instructional books can be produced by fishermen who write, whereas "devotional books" must be produced by writers who fish. Of course, good writers who are also sufficiently good fishermen may produce either or both, and both have value. The works that have no value, or at least hold no interest for many of us, are the superficial fish stories to be found on too many shelves. Especially in the devotional literature—those works categorized as "mood" books—the author has an obligation to formulate a philosophy as well as describe an experience. There is always the danger that the ideas may be trivial, or the philosophy too pedantically expressed. In these instances the mood book fails for angler and non-angler alike. Steve Raymond is too intelligent an angler, too gifted a writer ever to be guilty of such failure.

At its best, mood writing describes not only fish caught or fish lost but also a way of viewing life. As with any novel, the telling of a rapping-good story grabs the reader; the piece expresses the author's philosophy only in an unobtrusive way, almost subliminally. The ideas that ran like a barely noticed current in a trout stream linger sweetly when the story is finished.

Many angling books are so appealing that they are read by people who have no intention of ever chasing a fish. Perhaps no other sport can boast of such a rich literature. Examples range from *The Compleat Angler* by Izaak Walton to

*The Old Man and the Sea* by Ernest Hemingway (which are so very different in manner and content but which both celebrate the nobility of the fisherman).

The aforementioned *My Moby Dick* is another masterful example of an angling story that can be thoroughly appreciated by a far wider audience than those who fish. It was reviewed in *Newsweek* and sold exceptionally well not only in bookstores but in supermarkets, where one expects to encounter mysteries and romances but hardly a book about fly fishing. (And it can be argued that in our culture, success in the supermarket may well be the ultimate symbol of public acceptance.)

*The Year of the Angler* is a mood book infused with similar grace, intelligence, and broad appeal. There is a recurrent theme in Steve Raymond's writing: "In his searching, the angler sees many things. Often he is the first to notice change, because change always has meaning for an angler." In this book, the author marks time by the changing seasons. Each season has its own angling rituals. Somehow a sense of ritual can give order to one's life. A sadder theme in *The Year of the Angler* seems to be that personal rituals have no effect on the destructive changes assailing our world.

In his Preface, Arnold Gingrich compares Steve Raymond with other legendary writers of the Northwest; here let me simply add that he belongs to a select group of modern angling authors. He has the ability as a storyteller to bring the reader with him on the emotional roller-coaster ride, and at the end he lets us, as fly fishermen, celebrate our own nobility. *The Year of the Angler* definitely deserves its broad audience, for it does one thing more: it makes the angling life a bit more understandable to nonfishermen as well as fishermen.

—Gary LaFontaine

# Winter

The first fish of a new year is special in a way that all the rest are not. It may be a great, shining steelhead, taken on a cold, short January day from a pool surrounded by barren alders framed in ice, or a husky cutthroat, grown fat on humpback fry in a minor estuary in March, or a chunky rainbow from a landlocked lake in April.

Regardless of where and when it is taken, the details of the catch remain fresh in the mind, remembered after many other catches are forgotten. The first fish of a new year ends a subconscious suspense in the mind of a fisherman and becomes an omen that somehow sets the pattern for the remainder of the year.

The quest begins in winter, at the beginning of the year. And it seems strange that the year should be born then. It is a time when there is more darkness than light, more death than life, more silence than sound. In winter, the earth seems to draw into itself, resting from the business of having sustained life through the other seasons. The leaves are long gone from the forest limbs, the geese have flown in ragged arrows to the south and the roar of rivers is lost in drifts of snow along their banks.

Yet the rivers still harbor life, even in the frozen days of January. The last spawned-out salmon still thrash in the river shallows, while beneath the gravel the seeds of a new generation are growing. Steelhead, still bright from the sea, move upstream cautiously against the winter flow to seek their own spawning grounds. Close behind are the mysterious cutthroat in their own private, small tributaries.

Even so, winter ordinarily is not considered a time for angling. The gentleman trout fisherman hangs up his waders and his wicker creel and stores his fly lines in loose coils so they will be ready when the ice is gone and resident trout rise again in April or in May. His thoughts are of spring streams and summer rivers, and for him winter is merely a wait that must be endured before the changing of the season.

But there are other anglers who begin seeking their first fish of the new year on the first day, who wade the winter rivers and search them with a fly for steelhead. It is a long and sometimes painful search, and sometimes it goes on in vain until there is no longer a chance of finding fish in the river. It is a succession of long and fruitless hours spent in the rhythmic motions of cast and retrieve, of following the bright glimmer of the fly into the winter depths, of cheeks stinging in the cold and clots of ice forming in the rod guides.

The reward for all this effort sometimes never comes, because winter steelhead fishing with a fly is difficult indeed. But when and if it comes, it is dramatic and sudden: a quick, strong pull, the fleet feeling of helplessness as a heavy fish begins a long run or a high, shaking leap that somehow magnifies its size and strength. In a flashing moment, all the hours of effort and discomfort are forgotten in the sudden exhilaration of the strike, and total concentration is spent on the movement of the fish and the countermove of the angler.

That is winter steelheading: long hours of cold, interminable work, punctuated with breathless moments of high excitement. And if I were offered a choice of circumstances in which to take the first fish of a new year, I should prefer that it come in just that way.

# Hoh

January had come and gone and half of February had slipped away and there had been little opportunity for fishing. I had spent only a single day fishing in January, at a river close to home. It had been a bitter winter day, a day when it was necessary to wade through a thin layer of ice to reach the pools—a strange experience like punching one's way through a plate-glass window, taking care not to tear the waders on the splintered shards. It had been a day of hard work and no fish, and here in the middle of February I was still seeking my first fish of the year.

It was a cold, blustery morning when I left the city to

drive to the Olympic Peninsula. A southwester swept in ragged shreds of dirty cloud heavy with the promise of rain, and whitecaps slapped at the sides of the ferry as it crossed Puget Sound. It was still early in the day when I reached the Hoh.

Born in the Olympic snows, fed by the Pacific rains, the Hoh hurries down to the sea. In its high-mountain headwaters, the river is a precocious infant, skirting the base of glaciers, then growing as it absorbs the product of a hundred springs and tributaries, the rain forest runoff and the amber-stained water of the cedar swamps.

Hardly more than a brook at first, it grows quickly in size and strength and rumbles out of the mountains a full-fledged river with great sound and vigor and passes into the hushed canyons of the Hoh Rain Forest. From the forest it flows on to the brief coastal plain, dropping more gently now, restless in its passage, sprawling out and drawing in, seeking new channels as it passes through land scarred from logging. A short river as rivers go, it moves quickly from its source to where it meets the tide and is lost suddenly in the Pacific breakers.

In the summer the river carries the gray silt of its parent glacier, bleeding from the sun's wounds, and it never is without a trace of color from its source. The silt camouflages the quick movement of steelhead and salmon fry in the shallows. Deer slip silently from the forest to drink from the pools and eagles wheel in eccentric orbits overhead. When the fall rains come the river bustles with the life of returning salmon and cutthroat and the first bold vanguard of the steelhead run. It is a wild river, free and unrestrained, quick and exuberant and forever in hurried movement.

Winter comes slowly and subtly to the rain forest along the river. The first frosts leave a crimson rust on the vine maples, and the following wind sends dead leaves spiraling down to be swallowed up in the river.

One morning the higher hills are crowned with early snow, and as the days grow shorter and colder the snow creeps down to fill the higher valleys and the swamps are layered with ice. The lower valleys are hidden in a drenching gloom, coming down to settle in the forest itself, washing the tops of the highest firs and spruce.

The first big run of steelhead bursts into the river in December, struggling past the Indian nets at the river's mouth. They briefly rest in the quiet pools and pockets to restore themselves for the next frantic dash against the flow. The anglers know this, and seek them there, tempting them with strips of salmon roe or small bits of fiery yarn made fast to a hook; with bright nickel spoons and strangely shaped plugs and bobbers.

The fishermen wade out into the current or along the bars and cast with awkward grace, sending their unlikely offerings far out to be seized in the flow and sucked down, tumbled across the gravel and swept before the thrusting current, clumsily searching the places where resting steelhead lie.

The steelheaders come from everywhere, many with the river guides from the peninsula town of Forks. They bring their boats, stout McKenzies and sturdy Rogues, and trundle them down over the river rocks in the raining dawn. There is a sodden freshness to the morning that reaches through clothing and sets a man shivering, and the men talk in low voices in deference to the roar of the river.

The promise of rain had been fulfilled by the time I came to the river. The trees dripped moss and the moss dripped rain and the droplets formed rings on the river before the current snatched them away. It was still cold and the upper hills still held the snow so that the river was low and had only a trace of color.

The Hoh is a fisherman's river. There are pools and runs, pockets and slots throughout its length. Here a lone angler was plunking from the bank with a heavy bait rig, and there a pair of anglers fished from a boat in midstream. Fish were in the river and the river was right and it was a day in which a fisherman could feel confident that he would find fish if he looked long and hard enough.

I chose a spot where the river slowed and entered a broad bend, pausing midway to accept a small tributary, then broke in a riffle down to a large deep pool formed by an ancient log jam at its lower end.

There followed the familiar ritual of rigging up with all the accouterments that are a necessary part of the winter steelheader's uniform: the heavy wool socks, drawn up over the pair already being worn, and the whipcord trousers tucked in so there would be no bare expanse of skin between trousers and socks to touch the cold rubber of the waders. The waders themselves, chest-high, were cinched tight with a belt over a flannel shirt, a sweater and a heavy jacket.

And finally the vest, its many pockets sagging with fly boxes and all the other things an angler carries with him to the stream. And then the rod, a sturdy 8½-footer with a heavy, weight-forward, high-density fly line and a big reel filled with 150 yards of backing to follow the run of a strong fish; the leader, short and stout and testing at eight pounds; and finally the fly, a big one, size 1/0, with bright fluorescent chenille and a polar wing.

Thus equipped, I scrambled down a steep bank to the river's edge and worked upstream along the shore to the spot I had chosen to begin. It was hard going along a narrow path in the face of a cliff that dropped off sharply to deep water, then wading across the mouth of the tributary that had carved a respectably deep hole for itself where it entered the river. Finally I was able to walk out onto the shallow bar at the head of the drift and strip line off the reel for the first cast.

There is always a certain air of expectation about the first cast of a day of fishing. On rare occasions it is the very first cast that brings a smashing strike and wild excitement. And so

I was slightly tensed and slightly braced as I always am when I sent the first cast angling downstream. The fly floated momentarily and then disappeared as the current drew it under and swept it down into the deep water, and I saw it there in my mind's eye, the hackles swimming as it tumbled over and down and straightened out below me.

The current drew the line taut and the fly hung in the water, searching and seeking. After a proper wait, I drew it back, satisfied that this was not one of those days when the first cast would produce a rise.

I fished the water carefully, wading far out on the underwater bar until the waves lapped dangerously close to the wader tops. There was deep satisfaction in the graceful feel of the long rod, a sense of pleasure in watching the line roll far out, carrying with it the tuft of bright color that seemed so out of place in the darkening sky.

Nothing moved to the fly, and when I had covered all the water I could reach, I retreated from the bar and made my way downstream along the same hard path to the lower end of the river's bend, just above the riffle that carried down into the pool.

The water here was faster, pressing firmly against the waders until the cold could not be ignored. The sky dripped sporadically and the cry of a gull caused me to look up into the gathering rain. The river whispered and talked in a soft, low voice and seemed suspended in time and space, rushing out of the mist, flowing past and disappearing back into it. It was a time for thought, a time when the trained reflexes of the angler lead him to go on fishing while his mind turns to other things.

My mind was on the river, unique in some ways yet similar in others to all rivers. It was doing the things that all rivers do, moving the earth in tiny fragments, wearing down the hills, keeping the earth in a constant state of motion too slow for the human eye to see.

A river is like a man's life. It starts as a tiny, noisy thing, full of unchanneled strength and energy, a thing of unending movement. As it grows older and stronger it slows down a bit and begins to do important things, using its strength to dig canyons and fertilize flood plains with its silt. A few rivers, like a few men, do great things, carving monuments that are a wonder to the world. And also like some men, a few rivers create sorrow and disaster, bursting out of their channels with vicious strength to flood the fragile dwellings of men. But most rivers, like most men, pass quickly and are forgotten, having barely scratched the surface in their brief moment of time.

In their old age, rivers—again like men—grow ponderous and portly, spreading out and slowing down, always moving but somehow more reluctant now to go to their destiny. But finally the river flows across the last bar and is swallowed in the sea, quickly lost in all the waters that have gone before.

The fragments of matter the river has brought with it are scattered among the salts and minerals and flotsam of a thousand other rivers, and together they are mixed, separated and mixed again, driven by currents and carried by the wind to far shores. They are washed onto beaches in strange harbors, frozen into icebergs, drowned in the pollution of the coastal cities, and they are carried to the seven seas and the shores of all the continents. Water from all the rivers is drawn up by the sun's rays to condense and fall as rain on some distant watershed, there to seep into some distant river and begin the long cycle again.

Rivers breed legends, and the Hoh has one that seems appropriate for a river of its size and strength, a story about an extraordinary man who won for himself the name of the Iron Man of the Hoh. His real name was John Huelsdonk, a German immigrant who homesteaded on the river in the 1890s, and his great feats of strength as a logger, hunter and trapper quickly won him local fame. He was said to have killed more than a hundred cougars, including one huge, legendary cat known as Big Foot, and his great strength was attributed to the supposition that he ate the meat of the cougars he had killed. Huelsdonk survived a hand-to-hand fight with a black bear, an episode that made local headlines in the 1930s, and it was said he would pack 175 to 200 pounds of supplies on his back in order to earn two men's pay.

But perhaps the most appealing of all the stories about the Iron Man is one told by a forest ranger who said he encountered Huelsdonk packing a cook stove on his back down a forest trail.

"That must be quite a load," the ranger said.

"Well," the Iron Man replied, "the stove isn't so bad, but there's a sack of flour in the oven that keeps shifting around."

The Iron Man of the Hoh now is long dead, but there are other legends that linger on about the river. The Hoh flows into the sea between two great rocks that loom like monuments to its passage, and local Indian lore has it that these rocks once were animals that lived along the riverbanks. When they were told by the gods that humans were destined to come to the river, they chose to turn to stone, and there they remain as silent sentinels at the river's mouth.

The river now bears the name of a band of Indians that lived along its shores, but earlier in its history it was known as the Destruction River, so named by the captain of a ship who lost part of his crew in an Indian massacre at the river's mouth in 1787.

So the Hoh is a river rich in history and lore, and it is easy to understand how such tales were born and grew among the Indians and the early settlers who made their way through the dark and ghostly corridors of the great rain forest through which the river flows.

While my mind had been busy with these thoughts, I had fished down through the riffle to the point where it broke into the pool and cut its way far under the edge of the log jam, and there a sudden movement brought my attention back to the business at hand.

Deep in the pool there had been a quick flash near my fly, a fleeting image that had passed almost too quickly to discern. But it could have been a fish, and so I drew the fly back swiftly and cast again to the spot.

The current here was slow, and the fly was visible for a long time as it sank leisurely in the pool and was drawn toward the shadows of the overhanging logs, finally disappearing in the depths. And then came a hard jolt that pulled the rod tip down to the water, and slack line was whistling out through the guides until the line was taut to the reel and the sound of the reel's noisy ratchet echoed from the rocky banks.

Ignoring the refuge of the log jam, the fish moved quickly into the pool, heading downstream where the slack water of the pool was sucked out into a stretch of fast water. Once the fish reached that water it would be impossible to climb around the log jam to follow it, and so I tightened the drag on the reel and swung the rod around in an effort to turn the fish.

The fish broke water in a flash of gunmetal and silver, then turned and charged upstream through the pool. Now it was a matter of reeling quickly to recover the sudden belly of slack line forming below the fish. It ran past me and jumped again in the tail of the upstream riffle before the line was taut again against the reel. It was not an especially large fish, but it was strong and active and I wanted it badly.

Now it was back in the pool, twisting and shaking its head, and I could see the glint of its turning sides. Two short runs toward the tail of the pool set the reel buzzing again, and then the fish began edging toward the log jam where it had been hooked. The rod formed a tight bow against the raining sky as I put on as much pressure as I dared and kept the fish swimming parallel to the jam, away from its threatening snags.

And in a few moments more it was over and I edged the

fish carefully onto the gravel. It lay quivering on the wet stones, the fly stuck firmly in its lower jaw and a bright spot of blood on its lip. It was a fresh-run buck of seven pounds or better, clean and silver and strong, a classic example of a noble race, the brightest thing in the gray-painted day.

I crouched over it and twisted the fly free, then grasped the fish carefully and slipped it back into the pool, holding it upright until a throb of life returned and it swam slowly away, down and out of sight. It had given me all I wanted from it, and I had no good reason to take anything more.

I fished on without seeing another fish, and as the afternoon spent itself the drizzle ceased, the low clouds lifted to reveal the mountains overhead, and it grew colder. Finally, when it was time to go, my face was flushed with the cold and I felt an honest weariness.

As the truck rolled down the still-wet pavement, the sun broke through a higher overcast to paint the bold Olympics in changing pinks and golds, and the higher peaks became bright beacons to ships passing far out, a last soft sight of the dying day. I knew that behind that vast wall of mountains, two million lights soon would flicker on in the cities man has built on the banks of Puget Sound, signs flashing atop the great structures he has built to touch the low Pacific skies. All these works of man seem small and pale next to the silent majesty of the Olympics, the great thrusting shoulder of the continent, father of rivers, mysterious and unattainable even with great cities close at hand.

I leaned back in the seat of the truck and sighed with satisfaction. I had taken the year's first fish, taken it in just the way I would have wished, and it was bound to be a good year.

# The Quality
of Courage

Frozen patches of old snow lay here and there along the path leading down to the river. The day was cold and very still, and beyond the ragged tops of the surrounding firs and alders the sky had the strange white look that promised a new fall of snow.

I came out of the woods onto a broad gravel bar. On the far side of it flowed the river, dark and lazy in the cold gray light. I was hoping for a steelhead from the river, but as I started toward it a sudden movement caught my eye.

For a moment I was uncertain what I had seen. Looking around, I saw nothing except a small pool of water in the gravel at the edge of the woods, a pool that had been formed when last the river was in flood. The floor of the pool was lined with a soft carpet of decaying leaves, and a pair of downed alders lay across its surface. Beyond that there was only the gray and dun-colored gravel, the dusky green forest and the frozen sky.

And then I saw the fish. She was an old, spawned-out chum salmon, her once-handsome body now thin and scarred with fungus, and she had been hopelessly trapped in the little pool left behind by the flood. There was no telling how long she had been trapped there, and soon she would surely die as all Pacific salmon do after spawning. But she was still alert, and she had seen me coming, and it had been her quick movement of response that I in turn had seen. Now she was lying absolutely still in the shelter of the alder logs, and I had to look long and hard to distinguish her outline in the clear water.

I admired the fish. She had survived at sea and returned to find her native river, braved the pollution from the city on its banks, fought the freshets and floods to find this tributary, and finally she had spawned and fulfilled her duty to her race. And now she was trapped and dying in a lonely little pool, her courage and will to live intact to the very last.

I fished through the day, but stopped again at the little pool on the way back. The fish was there, still lying in the shelter of the log. For a moment I thought she was dead, but then I saw the slow movement of her gills and knew that she was not. I watched her for a while, and she watched me, and then I left, wondering if she would see the light of another morning. And I thought about the courage that had brought her so far and sustained her so long.

There is a great deal of courage in nature. A strong will to live is necessary for the species to survive, and each day wild creatures are tested anew in the cruel, efficient process of natural selection. The challenge of winter is met by different species in different ways. Some migrate to warmer places and new feeding grounds, some hibernate, and some change their habits to conform with the rigors of the season. The salmon survive in still a different way, the adults dying early in the winter after having laid eggs that will hatch in the spring to perpetuate the species.

The will to live extends to even the smallest creatures, the tiny mayfly nymphs clinging tenaciously to the undersides of rocks in the river's swiftest flow, the microscopic creatures of the plankton, breeding and dying, consuming and being consumed with the same determination to survive that is inherent in all the larger forms of life. The determination to live is so natural, so inbred, that usually it is accepted as a part of the natural scheme of things and only occasionally do we see it on display.

Once on a fall day when I was fishing a small lake in the Columbia Basin I saw such a display. It was a week after the opening of the hunting season and the surrounding hills resounded with the shots of duck and pheasant hunters. Three hunters had taken position in the cattails at the far end of the lake, and when an unwary mallard passed over all three stood and fired.

The mallard was hit and tumbled sharply in a shower of feathers, then caught itself and struggled gamely upward in erratic flight. It flew the length of the lake, but could go no farther and splashed lamely in the water close by, then swam ashore and dragged itself up into the grass.

All this had been visible to the hunters, but they made no move to retrieve the wounded duck. And when it became apparent they did not intend to do so, I went ashore and looked for it.

I found it, huddled and quivering in the bunch grass. There was no outward sign of injury, but when I picked it up the ground beneath was streaked with blood and I could see there were half a dozen holes in its belly. I stood there a moment, not really sure what I was going to do, and then the frightened mallard gave a sudden lurch and wrenched free. It stumbled to the water and made an awkward takeoff, struggling up from the water into clumsy flight. I watched its halting progress until it vanished over the next ridge. Surely it would not survive, but its will to go on living would be strong as long as life could last.

The determination to survive plays an important role in fishing. It is the will of the fish to live that causes it to struggle with all its strength against the restraining force of the angler. Fishing may be a matter of pleasure to the angler, and we think of it as such, but to the fish itself it is no less than a question of life or death.

Nearly every game fish that is in reasonably good condition will struggle valiantly for its freedom, but occasionally an angler will hook a fish that is unaccountably more violent than all the rest. Such fish test the angler's skill to its absolute limits, and regardless of the outcome the memory of the struggle remains vivid and clear.

One afternoon on a wilderness lake I hooked three such fish in succession. The day was well spent and I had taken many fish, but nothing had prepared me for the violence that followed. I covered a nearby rise and twitched the fly once and a trout had it. What followed was a stunning blur of motion: immediately the trout leaped, high and twisting, and was off and running almost before it hit the water. It was not an especially big fish—sixteen or seventeen inches—but it took yard after yard of line, then leaped high again and fell back on the leader, breaking it with an audible snap. The whole affair had taken only seconds and left me breathless and shaking.

I tied on a new fly and cast to the same spot. Another

trout, a twin of the first, took the fly and vaulted high in the air, shaking spray from its flanks. Six or eight times in succession it leaped with wild, reckless violence until the fly was wrenched loose from its fragile purchase in the fish's jaw.

Having lost two good fish in succession, I was now thoroughly rattled and spent a long moment in a conscious effort to calm myself, and to resolve that I would not lose the next fish if one was there. Two or three casts later another fish struck hard, and it too was wild, tearing long lengths of line from the reel, flinging itself out of the water in a series of twisting, inverted U's. I used every trick I knew to wear it down, and after a long fight it came in grudgingly until it was close enough to land. But as I reached for the net, the fish found strength enough to make a final, savage leap, shaking so violently that again the tiny hook tore out.

All this had occurred in less than ten minutes, but then the flurry ended. I was left with the knowledge that I had been beaten thoroughly by three splendid trout, wild things that deserved their freedom.

A defiant struggle for freedom and life is not the exclusive property of wild creatures. It belongs to men, too, though usually it shows itself in different ways.

I remember an old man I met once on a river, wading deep. His old frame looked too frail to stem the river's flow, but he waded boldly into the current, standing ramrod straight. His hair was white with age and his face leathered and burnt from countless days in the open, but his casts were swift and sure and he covered the water well. I admired him, much as I had admired the salmon in the pool, for his strength and courage had brought him a long way and he was not about to give up the sport he so obviously loved. Thinking of him now, I still see him standing in the river with such an air of quiet determination that I would not be surprised to return and find him standing there still.

There is no monopoly on courage. It is the quality of courage found in fish that leads men to fish for them. And it is something of the same quality in man himself that keeps him wading bravely through swift waters even when the hour is late and shadows are closing in around him.

# Bright Fly,
# Dark Fly

This was a happy river. It chuckled and talked as it spilled its way over shelves and ledges and broke into deep laughter as it slid into a turn at the foot of a steep cut bank. It was an exuberant river, rushing downhill quickly from its source as if anxious to reach a larger river and finally to reach the sea.

It was the best of winter days, and the air was clear and deeply cold, with a deceptively bright sun floating in a sky the color of a robin's egg. The sun painted shadows on the gravel bars along the river, using naked alders as its brush. The cold had kept the snow fastened to the hills so that the river was as low and clear as it would be again in late summer. Where the

water level had dropped along the banks it had left a gallery of
frozen art, with icy stalactites hanging from the lower limbs of
the adjoining forest. These too were struck by the sun, and
the light was fractured into a thousand rays of color. It was a
fresh day, a frozen day, a day when old storms were forgotten
and future storms seemed distant.

On such days the world stands out in bold relief. There
are no grays; only blacks and whites, brightness and darkness.
The river rippled out of sunlight into dark shadow, drove itself
into foam over the shallow, rocky stretches and resolved itself
into dark and quiet glides in the slower sections.

Even at low water, it was a fast river, and today the water
was very cold. There were steelhead in the river, but the low
water and strong light promised that the fishing would be
difficult and slow.

What fly to use? The bright, clear water seemed to call
for a bright fly. The cold water meant that the fish would be
deep and probably would be unwilling to move far to accept a
fly. These factors and the strength of the heavy current made
it mandatory that the fly be one large and heavy enough to be
fished well down. And so the choice was a bright pattern with
sufficient size and weight to search the depths of the faster
runs and pockets.

But what of the shadowed pools? Strangely it seemed as if
the sun were shining only on the fast water and the slower
stretches were bathed in deep shadow by the surrounding
forest. Here, perhaps, a darker pattern was called for, but
again the water temperature—and, in this case, the greater
depth—called for a fly that would sink even further. And so
the choice here would be a fly with a dark wing and a layer of
fuse wire around the body to carry it down.

Having made these decisions, I tied on the bright fly first
and waded in. The strong current curled around the waders
and built a wave on the upstream side, and I felt the familiar

pressure as the water compressed the air trapped inside the waders.

Every feature of the stream bottom was plainly visible in the strong light, and it was easy wading, even in the swiftest part of the flow. Here and there among the rocks I could see bright bits of yarn and broken bobbers, relics left by the bait and lure fishermen who had come earlier when the river was high. It was a small river, not the kind one thinks of as a steelhead river. There was no need here for the long cast, the double haul or the heavy rod. This was a roll-cast river, where the brush grew down close to the bank and it was but twenty careful paces through the current from one bank to the other.

The snow had come earlier, driven hard by the wind, clinging to the alders, gathering in the hollows, filling the network of crevices between the round rocks on the river bars. Then rain had followed, washing the snow from the limbs, and the runoff had come spilling out of the forest into the river in a thousand places. And then suddenly it had turned cold and the whole process had been frozen in a moment, and now the whole earth seemed still except for the river.

I started in at a spot where a mound of gravel split the river's flow, diverting a small part of it to one side and the larger part to the other. Where the larger flow skirted the edge of the opposite bank, it was busy gnawing its way into the network of roots and soil that marked the beginning of the forest.

And here it had made casualties of several maples and alders, whose dead limbs had fallen into the river. The run along the bank was deep, and the dead limbs provided an extra measure of cover. It was a natural place for steelhead.

Making short, careful roll casts, I dropped the fly in the small openings between the limbs and let it drift until another limb threatened, and in this unusual way I fished half the length of the run without result. And then I saw a fish, an old cock fish, working his way up from the lower end. He kept to the deepest water nearest the bank, moving up against the current a few feet at a time, pausing to rest under the protective cover of each downed limb, and it occurred to me that he was moving upstream in much the same way that I was fishing down.

I could see him clearly in the bright water. His belly and flanks were dark and there was a pronounced hook to his lower jaw. He was near to his spawning, less cautious than he otherwise would be, and I knew that had he still been a fresh fish I probably would not have seen him. My bright fly was swimming in a pocket above him, and I withdrew it to let him pass. It was doubtful he would have taken it at this stage of his migration, and in any case he needed his strength for another purpose and I had no need of him.

I left the fish to his difficult task, with a silent wish that he would be successful in his spawning and leave the river with a host of his progeny, and moved down to fish the water below.

I fished through a fast, deep run below a huge boulder, casting upstream to let the line sink and carry the fly deep through the hole, then fished through the tail of the run where hidden rocks revealed their presence by sudden boils in the current. Still nothing.

And then I entered the shadows and immediately it was colder. I changed then to the darker pattern, roll-casting to drop it near the far bank where the water slowed in a deep, mysterious pool. Half a dozen casts produced nothing, and then a hidden root deep in the pool seized the fly and held it so that finally it was necessary to break it free. I tied on another of the same pattern and moved downstream, where another deep run tailed off into a large pool, dark with shadow.

The first part of the run produced nothing, but midway through there came the sudden electric thrill of a strike and a large steelhead leaped, high and twisting, from the current. And in a split-second image that engraved itself on my memory I saw the fish, suspended in the spray of its leap, and the fly as it sailed clear of the steelhead's jaw. And in another second everything was just as it had been before, the current unbroken, the pool quiet, the line slack, as if nothing had happened.

No other fish came to the fly that day, and I hiked through the frosty thickets back to the car, thinking over the day's events. The bright fly in bright water had produced nothing, which was not surprising, because steelhead often seem reluctant to take under such circumstances.

The dark fly fished in the shadows had at least yielded a momentary connection with a fish. But had my choice of fly been made on valid premises? I had considered that the bright pattern would be easily visible in the strong light, but not so visible in the shadow. The darker pattern, I had reasoned, would show its silhouette in the shadow and thus be more readily visible there. A logical conclusion, no doubt, but with one important flaw: I had forgotten that fish are not necessarily logical animals, and they do not necessarily see or interpret things as humans do.

So many factors determine whether the fish takes the fly, and light is only one of them. Perhaps I had fallen into the old trap of following the traditional approach at the cost of trying something new that might have been more fruitful.

Bright fly, dark fly. So many theories surround the use of one or the other, and when the angler stops to consider them all, he begins to realize how little he really knows.

# Belfair

The sea trout of the Pacific Coast is the cutthroat, a nomadic wanderer of the estuaries. From the Alaska Panhandle to the Oregon shores, he moves in mysterious local patterns, probing now and then into the coastal streams, straying again into salt water, but never moving far from the mouth of a river.

Fishing the estuaries offers a change from the sound and swift movement of the rivers. In the estuaries, movement is slower and more subtle; the tide eases gently in and out, first touching, then covering the banks of eelgrass along the shore, then dropping quickly to reveal dark mudflats, mottled banks of gravel and crowded oyster colonies. In the estuaries there is nearly always a wind from the sea, a soft, sighing wind usually, sometimes gusting, and the graceful, dirty-white gulls balance on it and soar where it takes them, drifting as free and clear of the earth as a man's dream. The wind carries the scent of far places, of fish and kelp, of salt and distant rain, and it presses gently on the limbs of the windward timber, bending them into strange surrealistic shapes.

In all of nature, there is no place so rich in life as an estuary. The rivers bring a cargo of nutrients from the hills to mix with the abundant salts and minerals of the sea, and the tides flow back and forth in a great broth that breeds and sustains an infinite variety of life. The estuaries are plankton gardens, flashing with phosphorescent life by night, hosting the countless larvae of fish, crabs, barnacles and other creatures. Sticklebacks move in migratory swarms along with candlefish and herring and ugly sculpin in the shallows.

Steelhead and salmon move in and out, singly or in schools, searching for a familiar river, waiting for a freshet to bring water enough for them to make an ascent to their spawning grounds. Herons fish with quiet dignity along the shores; black brant and buffleheads make annual stops along their migratory routes; and occasionally harbor seals may be seen resting on the isolated, windswept spits. And in the midst of it all is the cutthroat, wearing the dark green of the forests on his back and the olive of the meadows on his sides.

Any good fisherman knows that it does not make good sense to seek the cutthroat in salt water. Finding him there is a very uncertain thing, because he literally has an ocean in which to lose himself. It is far more intelligent to fish for cutthroat in rivers, where they are confined to the limits of the river itself. Nevertheless, there is a strange attraction to fishing in salt water, because the search is an added challenge and when fish are found the pleasure is therefore greater.

There are many theories about where and when the cutthroat may be found and caught in salt water, and nearly all of them may be proved one day and disproved the next. The truth is that there is no pattern to the movements of cutthroat. They may come surging in schools when the rising tide comes boiling into the shallows, then linger long after the tide has ebbed; and then again they may not.

Cutthroats may follow the salmon into the rivers, trailing the spawning runs of cohos, pinks and chums, and indeed sometimes they do; but sometimes they do not. One school of thought holds that it is wise to look for cutthroats over oyster beds, and indeed often they are found there; and again, often they are not.

There is even uncertainty about the spawning time of cutthroats. Some say they spawn in November, others say in the winter; and a third group maintains they spawn in the spring. About all that may be said with certainty is that they do spawn, sometime, crowding into the little jump-across streams that run into the saltwater bays and sounds. And once having spawned, they may leave; and then again they may not.

Even in winter, when at least some fish are spawning, there are still bright fish along the beaches and in the bays, foraging for winter food. If the angler finds them, they will come willingly to the fly, and though they never reach extremely large size—four pounds would be exceptional—they are tough, stubborn fighters. Characteristically, the cutthroat fights in a series of strong, short rushes, taking maximum advantage of any underwater obstacle close at hand. And though they are not known as jumping fish, the only fish I have ever seen leap higher than my head was a sea-run cutthroat.

So this was the quarry that took five of us to Belfair on a rainy January day.

Belfair is a small town near the end of Hood Canal, a giant natural arm of salt water that runs north-south, dividing Washington's Kitsap and Olympic peninsulas, then doubles back in a deep stab of water pointed northeast toward Seattle. A dozen small streams run down out of the logged-off hills on the north shore of the canal, and it is a natural place for cutthroat.

A steady rain struck the water with a heavy hiss as we put up our rods and donned rain-repellent gear. Ed and Walt and I had brought cartop boats to explore the beaches; Doc and Syd were clad in waders to search the shallows off the creek mouths. The wind was only a faint stir, and the tide was sneaking in, reaching up for the driftwood scattered along the high-water line. It was the kind of day on which cutthroat seem to prowl.

Often we have found the cutthroat close to shore, in water so shallow it scarcely covers them. And so on this day we rigged up with floating lines in order to search the shallows without fear of hanging up on the eelgrass or the debris swept in by the tide. Each of us chose a bright fly, in keeping with the cutthroat's usual preference, and each of us tied on a light tippet to match the clear winter water.

The fishing technique is a simple one. One searches thoroughly, always watching for a telltale rise that may indicate the presence of a whole pod, or school, of fish.

And while searching, one also casts repeatedly, covering all the water around on the chance of hooking fish that may not have shown themselves. Anglers in boats follow the shoreline, casting in. Fishermen wading in the shallows also follow the shoreline, casting out.

So we set out to find the fish, Walt and I with our boats in the twin bays where creeks flowed in, Ed heading farther down the distant beach, and Doc and Syd wading along the shore. The canal was a broad expanse of dark water more than a mile wide, empty except for the black shapes of buffleheads rafted up far out. At the mouth of the nearest creek a swarm of gulls fed on the flesh of spawned-out salmon carcasses washed down from above.

We fished through the morning without seeing a single rise or sign of trout, indeed no sign of life at all except for an occasional grebe bobbing in the shallows. The rain never ceased, and soon it was necessary to pull the boats ashore and dump out the accumulated rainwater.

After noon, Walt and I broke for lunch, still fishless, and sprawled in the back of his wagon on the beach to eat our sandwiches. Ed still was out of sight, and Doc and Syd still waded, coming now and then into view through the swirling rain and gathering mist. The tide was almost at its height, sucking at the sand along the shore, reaching out for the row of flotsam left by the last high water.

We had nearly finished lunch when we heard Doc exclaim and looked up to see his rod bent sharply, the tip plunging in response to the frantic struggle of a fish. In a few moments, Doc had a handsome cutthroat on the gravel, a bright fish of about fourteen inches. "That, gentlemen, is what we came for," he said.

Encouraged, Walt and I returned to the boats and began searching the same water we had covered earlier. Still, there was no result, no sign of fish, and after a time our casts became mechanical and we had no real hope that a strike would be forthcoming. The tide was now at its highest, flooding up into the streams themselves so that their own identity was briefly lost in the intermingling waters.

And then there was a sudden rise in the small bay where we had fished so long and hard without seeing a prior sign of life. I cast toward the rise, and immediately there was a bulge near my fly, and I struck hard. There was a momentary resistance, and then nothing. Almost at the same moment came Walt's exclamation as he too missed a fish.

I cast again to the same spot, and this time there was no doubt. The fish took the fly firmly along the edge of the eelgrass, and I steered it toward open water as it struggled and turned. It fought with twice the vigor of a landlocked cutthroat, twisting and shaking and showing first one side and then the other, until I had it in the net, a twin of the trout Doc had taken earlier. And on the very next cast another fish took the fly boldly and struggled gamely before it came to the net.

But that was all. We fished the rest of the day without seeing another rise or fish. The tide and the day began their retreat simultaneously, the light ebbing along with the water. Ed returned from his trip along the beach with three small cutthroat on the seat beside him. We shed our drenched rain gear and packed up our rods, and Doc, Syd and Walt left for home while Ed and I went to dry out before the great stone fireplace at the nearby inn.

For most of the day the five of us had fished through the downpour, and we had only six trout between us. All the accumulated years of our angling experience, all the craft we had put into our flies, all the skill we could bring to bear had produced only six trout.

But that is the way of the sea-run cutthroat, a mysterious fish that moves in secrecy and silence along the beaches and the bays, vulnerable only to the most diligent searcher.

# Belfair
# Revisited

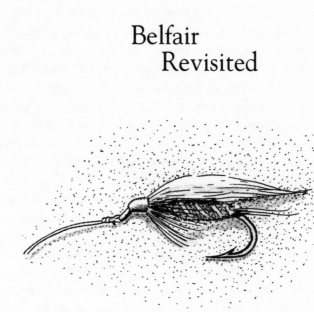

I have written of a typical day of sea-run cutthroat fishing, a cold, gray, wet day when the fish were few. Indeed, an angler has good reason to feel fortunate if he is able to take more than a few of these unpredictable trout in a day's fishing. Yet, even with the enigmatic cutthroat, there occurs an occasional, rare, red-letter day when all goes well, when the fish come quickly and easily, even though conditions do not seem completely right.

I have fished often near Belfair, but only one such day has come to me there. There was nothing about it to set it apart from many other days in the estuaries, except that on this particular day the trout seemed to lack their usual cautious ways and accepted eagerly any fly I offered them.

Less than a week earlier the canal had been frozen solid enough for a man to walk across it. The fresh water draining down from the creeks and small rivers had frozen in a layer upon the salt water, and it had stayed that way until warming temperatures and a strong wind had broken it up with splitting sounds like pistol shots. The wind had carried away the broken shards of ice, and the ice had taken with it many of the docks and floats built by cabin owners along the shore.

The ice was gone when Ed Foss and I reached the canal, but frozen drifts of snow were still in evidence along the shore. A steady south breeze sent waves sliding up the gravel beach, and rain mixed with snow spattered on the hoods of our rain parkas.

The tide was rushing in, piling up over the eelgrass and the oyster beds, slapping against the concrete seawall by the old house on the point. Smoke rose from the fireplace chimneys of a dozen cabins, but the beaches and the water were empty except for the usual buffleheads and gulls.

We unloaded our boats from Ed's truck and carried them down the beach to the water's edge, then rigged up our rods and lines. It was nine a.m. when we started fishing, obeying the old adage that the best time to fish for sea-run cutthroat is just before the high tide, which was at ten. We fished along the shore of the first shallow bay, a place where we had seldom failed to find at least a few scattered cutthroat, but at this hour there were none in evidence. Slowly we worked our way to the tip of the far point, where a small stream runs into the canal. We reached it at high tide, when the salt water reached far into the creek mouth, and cast over the oyster beds at its mouth. Still, there was no sign of fish. We had been fishing more than an hour, and it was beginning to appear as if we were in for another day of long searching and few trout.

A great bald eagle suddenly broke cover from the brush

near the old house on the point and took flight on long, graceful wings. We watched as it flew more than a mile distant, still plainly visible, until it settled in the top limbs of the tallest tree on the next point.

Now the tide was changing, and the wind and the tide were at war with one another. The waves swept in by the breeze fought the outgoing tide, setting up a tidal rip along the edge of the point. Sometimes the cutthroat will come to feed in the rips, searching out the food organisms tossed about by the contending waters, but Ed fished through the rip carefully and there was no response.

Then we separated, and Ed headed farther up the beach while I elected to return to the bay we had fished earlier. The water was as clear as I had ever seen it, and each oyster shell and colored rock stood out boldly on the bottom. I cast into the beach where the water scarcely covered the gravel, then cast outward into pockets sometimes five or six feet deep. But there was not a single rise, nor any sign of fish.

At one time there had been two old pilings standing in the bay, and it seemed as if there always were cutthroat somewhere around them. But then the pilings had disappeared, pulled out, I suppose, by the landowner whose property they fronted. After they were gone the fishing became much less certain, but still I searched the old area thoroughly, casting in and out, working the fly shallow and deep, fast and slow. And still there was no response.

I moved farther back into the bay and stopped at a place where a small stream carried the runoff from the melting snow down over the gravel beach, through a patch of eelgrass and into the canal. It was such a tiny flow as to hardly qualify as a stream, scarcely enough water to wet one's boots.

Casting in, I probed the area along the beach where the streamlet flowed in. It was nearly eleven o'clock, and in two hours of fishing I had not seen a sign of trout. But then, without any forewarning, there was a strong take, and I was fast to a good cutthroat. He plunged and turned and sought the bottom, and I tried to steer him into deeper water. Even as I did so, there came a rise near the spot where I had hooked him, followed closely by a second rise nearby, and I knew I had found a school of feeding cutthroat.

I netted the first fish as quickly as I could, anxious now to make another cast before the school moved on. The first trout was bright and fat, about one and a half pounds, with deep crimson slashes underneath its jaws and an iridescent olive gleam to its flanks.

I removed the fly and cast again toward the rises and immediately hooked a second fish, followed quickly by another on the next cast. In years of cutthroat fishing, I have learned never to expect to take more than two or three fish from a school before it moves on, so I hurried my casts, hooking fish, playing them and releasing them as quickly as I could. The tide was dropping rapidly and I felt sure that the school would move out into deep water.

Yet strangely, it stayed where it was, the rises continued, and I continued to catch fish. I looked for Ed, but he was still far off down the beach, out of hailing distance.

I did not know what food had brought the cutthroat to this place, but they responded willingly to my fly. It was an old pattern called an Omnibus, with a body of peacock herl, a red-and-yellow hackle and a bucktail wing. It was the invention of Lendall Hunton, a banker who developed the pattern in the estuaries of Willapa Bay, and it was a proven taker of cutthroat. But I had only two of them in my fly box, and soon the cutthroat chewed them both to shreds. So I switched to another pattern, and it made no difference.

Now the trout were rising almost as if a mayfly hatch were on the water, and one fish jumped clear of the surface to fall upon my fly. It was the type of fishing I have come to know and expect in lakes when a heavy hatch is on, but it was completely unexpected on a winter day in salt water.

Ed now was rowing toward me and I hailed him and told him to come alongside. He anchored his boat nearby and began fishing. Ed is a veteran cutthroat angler who fishes with great skill; he also was using an Omnibus, casting to the same spot, retrieving in the same way. But as sometimes happens, all the luck was with me that day, and none with him. I continued to hook cutthroat, but the trout ignored his fly. Finally he had a strike, fought the fish and landed it—and it turned out not to be a cutthroat, but a small silver salmon.

For two hours the trout rose in the same spot and we fished for them there until the tide dropped so far down it seemed our boats soon would go aground. When we quit fishing and started rowing back to Ed's truck parked on the beach, I had caught more than twenty cutthroat, all of them strong, bright and unusually heavy fish. Nearly all of them had been returned to the water, but I had kept a few in order to examine their stomach contents.

That night I did so, digging out preservative formula, collection bottles, identification keys and a strong magnifying glass. The trout stomachs were filled with several species of shrimp and with aquatic sow bugs. Scale samples, studied under the microscope, indicated the fish all were entering their third year of life, and I assumed that their larger brethren had been busy with spawning on this February day.

Since then I have fished at Belfair other times, and the fishing always has been what it was before that memorable day—long hours of casting and searching, with only a few trout to remember at the end of the day. But since that one occasion when the trout came so frequently and well, I always go there with the hope that there will be another such day. And someday, I know, there will be.

# A Choice
of Method

I should like to know something about the man who first thought of luring a fish with an artificial fly. I should like to know something of his motives, and of what he felt in that exciting moment when his grand experiment was successful.

I would like to think that he was a visionary man, and that in the moment of success he had some inkling of the significance of the event, some glimmer of knowledge that one day many thousands of anglers would fish in the tradition he established on some long-forgotten river.

Whoever this man was, he must have been a keen student of the life of rivers to have perceived the subtle relationship between the fish and the fly. I wonder if his knowledge went beyond that, and whether he also knew something of the relationship between the sun, the wind and the water, the plants of the river and the insects that feed upon them, and of the relationship between the fish and man himself. If he knew all this, then he truly was a perceptive man, because even today there are few who know it.

Most anglers regard their relationship with the fish as a competitive one, and when they succeed in outwitting the fish they consider they have won the competition. This is a false view of the way things really are. Whether man realizes it or not, the true nature of the man-fish relationship is one of cooperation, not competition. The man is dependent upon the fish and the fish is dependent upon the man, just as all life is interdependent.

What this means in the modern context is that the angler must give up the old idea that trout or salmon are crops to be harvested. With so many fishermen and so many fewer fish, there is a danger that soon there will be nothing more to harvest.

Modern technology has addressed the problem in a different way. If runs of fish are endangered by overfishing, by pollution or by dams, technology's answer has been to raise them artifically in hatcheries so the numbers of fish may be maintained or even increased.

But this is not a solution. There is very little natural selection in a hatchery. The weak survive as well as the strong, and the whole race suffers as a result. The genetic qualities that have made each strain of fish uniquely suited to its native river are quickly erased in hatcheries. Evolution always has been been a trend from the random to the specific, but this trend is reversed in the hatchery.

Hatchery fish may still provide a quality of sport sometimes equal to their wild counterparts. But there will be subtle differences in their behavior—in the time of their return to the river in which they were stocked, in the time spent ascending the river, in their response to temperatures and flow, in other ways. They are not fully in harmony with their environment, as a native fish would be. And that is one reason why wild, native trout and salmon are today so valuable, and why the angler has little right to remove them and their precious source of genetic material.

This is not to say that an angler has no right to keep or kill his catch. Some strains of fish have overpopulated, and in such cases the fisherman does the whole race a favor when he keeps his catch. And the hatchery fish are meant to be harvested; in fact, are considered in terms of economic crops by the agencies which produce them. But the angler should be careful when he is fishing for wild fish, lest he assist in the destruction of something that, once gone, never will be seen again.

Man is so used to the idea that he enjoys complete dominion over the earth that only recently has he given much thought to the consequences of some of his actions. Still, in the literature of angling, there is evidence that from time to time some fishermen have questioned the wisdom of removing trout or salmon from their native waters, and some have gone so far as to construct elaborate justifications for it. Perhaps the most imaginative and amusing of them all is that set forth by William Scrope in *Days and Nights of Salmon-Fishing in the Tweed* in 1843. Scrope says:

"Let us see how the case stands. I take a little wool and feather and tying it in a particular manner upon a hook make an imitation of a fly; then I throw it across the river and let it sweep around the stream with a lively motion. This I have an undoubted right to do, for the river belongs to me or my friend, but mark what follows. Up starts a monster fish with his murderous jaws. It makes a dash at my little Andromeda. Thus he is the aggressor, not I; his intention is evidently to commit murder."

And so, if Scrope may be taken seriously, he would have us believe that it is the fish who is at fault, and the poor angler is merely defending himself. But there were a good many more salmon in the English waters of Scrope's day than there are now, and one wonders what his attitude would be now.

The next logical question for the reader to ask is, what is the use of fishing if one should not always keep or kill his catch? The answer to that, as many anglers have found, is that there is much more to fishing than merely catching fish. There is more excitement and more accomplishment in the stealthy approach, the careful cast, the gentle float of the fly and the slashing rise of the fish than there is in killing the fish after it has been subdued and may no longer struggle for its freedom. Indeed, killing the fish is an incongruous act after all the preparation and effort that has gone into the deceiving and the hooking of it.

That is why fly fishing is so important, and it is one reason why I have adopted fly fishing as my own method. The experienced fly fisherman knows that the method is more important than the result. And if the result is successful, as it often is, then he has the option of returning his catch to the river with little risk of injury.

There is nothing sacred about fly fishing, although so much has been said and written about it that it has acquired nearly the status of a religion. There is really nothing important that sets it apart from other methods except the attitude of the practitioner. Indeed, fly fishing is more nearly defined as a philosophy than a method, and the philosophy should include tolerance of other methods, so long as they do not endanger the resource held in common by all anglers.

But it is very difficult to explain this philosophy to people who fish with the sole objective of bringing home their catch. They do not understand that it is possible to measure success in other ways.

I have mentioned the difficulty of taking winter steelhead on a fly. The winter fly fisherman knows that his chances of success are small, that the odds are stacked against him. And yet there are many who fish through the winter with nothing but a fly.

Why do they do it? Obviously there is something more involved than a simple desire to catch fish. The winter fly fisherman may measure success in terms of the sights and sounds of a winter river, or the sense of pleasure he receives from sending his fly on a long cast across the swirling current to a steelhead lie on the distant side of the river. Or it may be nothing more than the chance to breathe the clean, cold air of winter, to feel the rush of current against his waders and the solid feel of gravel underfoot. The angler may come home fishless after a long day on the river and still feel he has been denied nothing.

Admittedly, this is still an uncommon attitude, but it is growing in the face of reality. There is slow acceptance of the idea that if a man does not practice conservation in sport, he is not likely to practice it in other ways, and when the equation is carried out to the very end he finds that it is really his own habitat that he is trying to conserve.

And so the lesson is that man and the fish must co-exist, that the angler should use the resource but not use it up, that success need not be measured by the number of the kill, and that every care should be taken to guard the wild heritage of salmon and trout so that these best examples of nature's work shall not vanish from the earth. And fly fishing, with all its other inherent pleasures, is the method—and the philosophy—most consistent with this noble purpose.

# Waiting for
## Winter's End

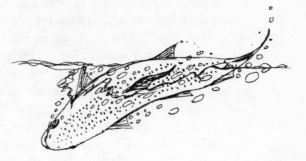

Winter ebbs in March. The crackling cold of January and the February frosts are past, and the earth shrugs and begins to awake from the long night of winter.

The southwesters begin sweeping up the Narrows, piling smoky surf on the beach in front of the house, driving the rain hard against the windows like fistfuls of buckshot. The nights still are long and often stormy, but the days are warmer and there is an imperceptible stirring of life in the forests and the fields.

The steelhead are fewer now, and though March may be a prime month for cutthroat, the weather often is inhospitable to fishermen. There is a raw violence to the storms that mark the changing of the season, the labor pains of the renewal of life.

When March arrives, the opening of the trout season is not far away and there always is much to be done to prepare for it. And so in March I fish less often, preferring to spend the blustery evenings next to the warmth of a blazing hearth, tying leaders and flies, wrapping rods, looking after the equipment that soon will be used to test the trout in the lowland lakes.

It always is necessary to tie new leaders, and a couple of evenings are spent with tape measure and micrometer and spools of material in various diameters. And usually it is time to replace the guides on a favorite rod, and out comes the winding silk and varnish until the job is done. But most of all, there is a need to tie flies, to replenish the supply that dwindled in the last season when flies were left on overhanging limbs or underwater snags, given away to other fishermen or left in the jaws of fish that would not be restrained.

A fly tier is an artist. The pelts of exotic birds and animals are his paints and the hook is his palette. He uses a vast and varied assortment of materials—steel hooks forged in England or Norway, fur from the belly of a red fox or a hare, hackles from the neck of an Indian gamecock—and binds them all together with natural silk to create his impression of a living insect. His work is subjected to an eye far more critical than that of any human reviewer—the sharp, wary eye of the trout.

The number of fly patterns is infinite. Usually the novice tier develops his skill on old and tested patterns, then moves quickly on to his own designs. And, just as each artist has a different view of the world, so each fly tier sees things in his own special way. The result is many different patterns, even though the number of insect types on which trout are known to feed is relatively small.

The concern of the trout fisherman must be with those

patterns that imitate the nymphs, larvae and pupae of aquatic insects or their winged adult stages, plus the many and varied terrestrial insects that live along the shores of rivers. But the fly-tying trout fisherman has gone beyond that to create imitations of small forage fish and minnows and a host of "attractor" patterns that bear no resemblance to anything in nature. And there are still other patterns, created especially for a single species, such as the delicate, beautiful Atlantic salmon flies, the gaudy patterns used for sea-run cutthroat and steelhead and the new generation of flies for saltwater species.

Many anglers have a few favorite flies they will fish with confidence under any circumstances. In fact, looking back over my own records, I see that I have taken more trout on a nondescript nymph pattern than on any other single fly. Though the pattern never was meant to imitate a specific insect, it seems to have something that makes it appealing to trout. Looking further, I see that it has been about equally effective for rainbow and brook trout, but almost a total failure for Kamloops trout—for reasons I cannot fathom.

I have taken many cutthroat on a fly with a body of hot-orange chenille, suggestive of nothing found in nature but in keeping with the strange preference cutthroat seem to have for bright and gaudy colors. And although my box of steelhead flies is filled with a grand assortment of patterns, the old Skykomish Sunrise overshadows all the rest in effectiveness.

It is all very well for an angler to have favorite flies, but he must always fish with an open mind and be willing to try the untried if he is to be a consistently effective fisherman. Sooner or later he will encounter a hatch or some set of conditions in which his old favorites will prove to be of little value, and then he must be willing to depart from established procedure. This seems obvious, but anglers—especially fly fishermen—are a strangely conservative lot and often they insist that the fish meet them on their own terms, an attitude which is not likely to result in many fruitful days.

Though I try to tie enough flies in winter to last through

the trout season, I discovered long ago that on extended trips
it is wise policy to take along at least a minimum amount of
fly-tying gear in case a new pattern is needed to match local
hatches or conditions. Some of my most effective patterns
were first tied under such circumstances.

In particular I remember an occasion at Leighton Lake in
British Columbia. It had been an unseasonably warm spring
and when we arrived late in May the fish already had been
driven deep by the heat. Leighton is one of the richest of the
British Columbia lakes, with a vast abundance of shrimp,
snails, chironomids, sedges and nymphs of damsel and
dragonflies. But despite the heat, the hatches still were sparse
and it was impossible to tell what the trout were seeking in
their deep feeding. Neither I nor other anglers could find a
consistent fly.

Finally I took a decent trout and examined its stomach
contents. It had been feeding very selectively on damselfly
nymphs of a pale translucent green, unlike anything I had in
my fly box. So I mounted a tying vise on the seat of my boat
and went to work, experimenting with silks and feathers and
furs until I had devised an imitation that seemed reasonably
close in color and shape. Armed with a pair of the new flies, I
returned to fishing and took six Kamloops trout in the next
hour, all bright, strong and wonderfully active fish. And in
the ensuing years that pattern first tied on the shore of
Leighton Lake has proved to be one of the most effective I
have used whenever damselfly nymphs are active in the
spring.

Over the years, I have kept rather careful records of the
effectiveness of the fly patterns I have used, a practice which
has yielded valuable information and more than a small share
of pleasure. The figures and the names of the patterns and
places transform themselves into memories of spring or
autumn days, of far-flung lakes and rivers, of Colorado's
Roaring Fork surrounded by the mantle of the season's first

snow and the slow, sweet water of Silver Creek amid the bare hills of Idaho. One notation reminds me of the incredible hatch on the Henry's Fork, another of the day the flying ants flew in clouds over Hihium Lake. Here is the record of my first salmon, and there the one for the first wily brown enticed from the Madison.

October always has been my favorite month for fishing, and it always seems to me that I do best then, but my own figures prove me wrong. The record shows that September actually has been the best, and July, surprisingly, is second. October is only third, and I suspect it is because October fish are larger and more difficult and I remember them better that October always seems the best.

There are other things to do in the dying days of winter besides tying flies and mending rods. Perhaps the most enjoyable pastime of all is looking through the many tackle and fly-tying catalogs that come in the mail. It seems they come in every month of the year, and pile up unopened until there is time in the winter to leaf through them and take note of the old, the new and the unusual.

Of them all, one of my favorites is the little book from Rogan of Donegal, Ballyshannon, County Donegal, Ireland. It isn't much as catalogs go—lists of flies printed on only one side of thin, tissuelike pages. But the name itself has a good, Irish richness to it, and somehow it always makes me think of a steaming mug of thick Irish coffee on a frosty morning.

But the name is not the only unusual thing about this little catalog. It is the only one I know that offers only hand-tied flies—flies tied without the aid of a vise. This method is a difficult and dying art in which the tier holds the hook between his thumb and index finger throughout the tying process.

As the catalog itself states, "This method of tying which was developed and perfected by three generations . . . ensures the correct tension on the tying silk, eliminates local stress on the hook caused when using a bench vise, and produces a uniform fly of great durability."

I can't testify for the durability of Rogan's flies, but I can vouch for their beauty and perfection. I first saw the catalog when I was given a copy by Doc Musgrove, who then was president of the fly-fishing club in the Seattle suburb of Edmonds where I had gone to give a talk. It seems he had made a wager with a friend that it was impossible to tie a fly smaller than size 16 without using a vise. Doc had seen an advertisement for the hand-tied flies of Rogan and had written to the firm in hopes that it could provide evidence to settle the wager in his favor. Back came a small package with a size-18 Royal Coachman and a letter advising that the fly indeed had been tied without the aid of a vise. Not only that, but the tier apologized for the fact that he had been out of size-22 hooks or he would have sent a hand-tied fly in that size.

I examined the fly under a magnifying glass and found it perfect in every detail, at least the equal of any fly I have ever seen come out of a vise. Doc lost his wager, but he introduced a number of us to Rogan's quaint catalog.

Another favorite is the catalog from E. Veniard Ltd., which includes perhaps the most complete list of fly-tying materials available anywhere.

As John Veniard wrote in the introduction to the 1970 catalog, ". . . our aim is to supply the needs of the amateur fly-tyer at a reasonable cost commensurate with the highest standard of quality and service, and although in some instances our prices may seem to be a little high, this is amply compensated by the fact that everything purchased by our clients is usable. In other words, all 'rubbish' is excluded. . . ."

Veniard's well-illustrated book is indexed so that one may quickly turn to the item he is searching for. It has the most complete line of tying vises I have seen anywhere, including a hand-held model. And I don't know of another place where one could order such items as "the 'Peter Deane' Fly Tyers' Bottle Stand," the "Hills Patent Cast Carrier" or a "fluorescence detector."

Of the many American catalogs, my first choice is that of William Mills & Son. It offers nothing but fishing tackle and accessories and doesn't clutter its pages with extraneous items aimed at catching the eye of a fisherman's wife. And, of course, it features the great H. L. Leonard rod, along with an illustrated explanation of how the rod is made.

The Orvis Co. catalog probably is the most colorful of all, and though it advertises many items that have little interest for anglers, the publishers have had the good sense to put their fine bamboo rods right up in front. And there also are large selections of flies, fly-tying materials and books for window-shoppers such as I.

Then there is the Abercrombie & Fitch catalog with its Bogdan, Seamaster and Fin-Nor reels and its fine mahogany tackle boxes; and Anglersmail with its wide selection of rods—R. H. Woods, Sharpes of Aberdeen, and Leonard—and of British and American flies and books.

Less known but just as interesting is the newspaperlike catalog of the Brule River Tackle Supply. It offers nothing out of the ordinary in the way of tackle, but has a complete selection of snowshoes, along with some unusual items such as Steen's Pure Ribbon Cane Syrup and Black Duck Wild Rice.

And there are so many others—the Rangeley Sport Shop; Bud Lilly's; Arthur L. Walker & Son Fly Reels; Vince Cummings Rods; Harrington & Richardson, with its line of Hardy rods and reels; L. L. Bean, Inc.; Eddie Bauer, and on and on, each one a separate treasure trove of tackle and accessories. Among them are two that deserve special mention—the Wretched Mess Gift Catalog, and Herter's.

The first of these offers a strange assortment of odds and ends compiled by Dave Bascom, better known as Milford (Stanley) Poltroon. Poltroon has gained a dubious sort of fame

with his zany magazine, *The Wretched Mess News*, a "piscato-
rial periodical" devoted to satire and slapstick about fish and
fishing.

It's probably safe to say there is no other catalog that
offers, in addition to rods and flies, a book entitled *How to
Conquer Stupidity*; a Venus flytrap plant; or dog, cat and
husband tags. It's also probably the only catalog that allows
the customer to buy everything in it for one lump sum.

Herter's is notable because it's the largest outdoor
catalog, and also because of its old-fashioned text and
endorsements from satisfied customers. There are a lot of
unusual items in Herter's catalog, but perhaps the strangest of
all is "Herter's Ancient Passenger Pigeon Decoys." They must
have been effective, because the passenger pigeon long ago
was rendered extinct by overhunting as well as by destruction
of its habitat. As the catalog says: "Not too long ago the
passenger pigeons were very plentiful. A few passenger pigeon
decoys hung up in a tree would bring flock after flock. The
Herter women would go to the decoy tree and pick up the
dead pigeons in their aprons and walk back to the house to
clean them. Passenger pigeons were nothing special to eat as
they were dark fleshed and a little livery. But well flavored
with onions they were not too bad, especially if you had a lot
of children to feed."

Perusing catalogs is an entertaining pastime, but it
doesn't compare with angling. And when the last catalog is
closed, the last fly is tied, and the last winter storm has blown
itself out, it is time for Opening Day—time to go fishing
again.

# Spring

In the spring, the rainbow and Kamloops trout spawn, and always it is exciting to watch this ritual in the small tributary streams. The larger rivers are often in freshet with runoff from the winter snows, and the steelhead and salmon fingerlings ride to sea on the wings of the flood. The forests and fields bloom with fresh life, and in the heat of the day the insects hatch and the trout in the lowland lakes begin to rise. The mornings are cool and fine, the evenings grow long with gentle, dying light, and everywhere there is new life and renewed life.

I have seen many seasons pass since that first spring trout

took my fly, but I still remember it well. My father had come home from the war and together we made the long, exciting trip into the British Columbia interior, a strenuous journey in those days. Finally we turned off what then was the main road and started up a pair of ruts into a grove of tall aspens. The silver leaves twinkled where the sunlight caught them until finally we were above them and into a stand of lodgepole pine. Here and there we passed cleared fields rimmed with split-rail fences where white-faced Herefords grazed. And then at last we came to a tiny tributary stream that flowed into the lake that was our destination.

The stream was hardly two feet wide, with an even flow of cold springwater over a fine gravel bottom. It was jammed with spawning Kamloops trout, some longer than the stream was wide, some so thick the water scarcely covered them.

It was the first time I had seen spawning fish, and we lingered at the stream to watch as the scarred males fought one another for supremacy and the females thrust their tails into the gravel to make nests for their spawn. Perhaps it was then that I first realized what hardships a trout must overcome to be born in the river gravel, to survive and grow, to return and spawn, and what a miracle it is that they are able to overcome them.

Then we went on to the lake, and the next morning it was bordered with thin ice before the sun was full upon the water. The sky was a brilliant blue, and beyond the dark pine forest on the far side of the lake the mountains still were crowned with snow. It was a scene of bright beauty and freshness that made the whole earth seem new and clean. And then came the fragrance of burning alder as fires were started in the cookstoves, and soon the aroma of frying bacon was mixed with the warm, pleasant scent of the alder smoke.

After breakfast we started out on the lake, and my father handed me a fly rod and showed me how to trail the fly behind the boat. Soon I felt the sudden wrench of a hard strike, a feeling that was to become familiar over the years, but one which still never fails to generate something of the same excitement I felt in the moment of that first violent pull.

The trout was not a large one, but it leaped gamely and I quickly thrust the rod into my father's hands so that he could play and land it. Even so, I thought of it as "my" trout, my very first, because I had been the one who had hooked it.

A good many years have passed since that event, but the bright visions of those early days are with me still, and I am grateful for them. And each April, when the trout begin to rise again, I go out with something of the same feeling, and I suspect that no matter what his age, each fisherman becomes a small boy again in the spring.

# The Trout
## Under the Cedar Limb

It was a day typical of April, bright but cool, with a stiff breeze sweeping in through the timber from the south, riffling the water of Pass Lake. A late snowstorm in the mountains had forced the cancellation of a planned trip east, so at the last moment I had decided to return to Pass Lake, where only the previous weekend the members of the Washington Fly Fishing Club had gathered for their annual Opening Day celebration.

Pass Lake is perched on the high shoulder of Fidalgo Island in Puget Sound, overlooking the great chasm of Deception Pass where saltwater tides rip in and out with awesome speed and force. The lake itself is surrounded by tall timber and lush pasture, kept that way by conservationists who waged a long fight to save it from a massive real-estate development. The lake is shallow and rich and restricted to fishing with the artificial fly. It is kept heavily stocked with rainbow trout so that no angler, even the most clumsy, need go home empty-handed. Usually there are more trout than the lake can comfortably support, so that the average size is not large. But each year there are a few fish that survive until the next season, and of that number there are again a few that hold out for a third year and grow to a respectable size. Two-pounders are not really uncommon and occasionally a lucky angler will hook a really heavy fish of four pounds or better.

But on this particular day, Pass Lake was not eager to yield its trout. The water was cold from a winter that had held on more persistently than most, and the angling pressure during the season's first week had been heavy so that the trout were both sluggish and wary.

I fished in all the usual spots with all the usual flies and released several small fish and a single dark two-pounder, but the action was slow compared to the usual standard. And then, as I let my boat drift down the lake on the gathering breeze, I noticed a cautious rise close to shore, followed quickly by another. It was not a place where I usually fished; in fact, it was a place that most anglers seemed to ignore. But on such a day as this, when the trout were not coming easily, nothing could be overlooked.

Maneuvering close to shore, I watched and waited to see what had prompted the rises I had seen. And there it was: the pupal shuck of a small chironomid bobbing to the surface, the adult fly struggling to free itself, then drying its wings in the open air as the wavelets carried it away. Studying the water, I noticed others hatching, so I traded the sinking line and nymph pattern I had been using for a floating line and a dry fly tied to imitate the chironomid adults.

On the first cast the fly cocked nicely and rode up one side of a small wave and down the other before it disappeared quickly in a swirl. I raised the rod and was fast to a fish, but it was not a large one. I brought it in quickly, twisted the fly free from its jaw and watched it dart away. Two others quickly followed, but neither was large and I was hoping for some bigger game.

And then I saw a quiet rise far back under the overhanging limb of an old cedar growing at the edge of the lake. The limb sagged under its own weight, the foliage dragging in the water. There was no way to cast directly to the spot without hanging the fly in the foliage. I dried my fly and studied the situation, trying to think of a way to reach the trout. The rise had left me with the impression that this might be a bigger fish, and there was confirmation in the well-sheltered spot chosen by the trout as its feeding station.

As I watched, I saw another chironomid pop to the surface and begin to struggle out of its pupal shuck, and as it did so the breeze carried it slowly back under the cedar limb, where it disappeared in a careful rise that was a duplicate of the first one I had seen.

Perhaps, I thought, I could use the wind in the same way, letting it carry my artificial to the trout. I cast ahead of the limb and threw extra slack line on the water, then waited while the breeze slowly carried the fly back into the shadows beneath the cedar limb. But the cast had not been long enough and the fly swung around short of the spot I was aiming for. A second cast, with more line, and another wait, and this time the wind carried the fly precisely to the spot. There was a rise, the fly disappeared, and I raised the rod gently to set the hook. The water erupted and a fine trout leaped, shaking itself and nearly striking the limb overhead. Just as quickly, the line went slack as the fly pulled out. It was easily the largest trout I had ever hooked in Pass Lake, and, as it turned out, the last large fish I was to hook that day.

A week later I went back to try again. The conditions were much different; this time the sky had the iron-gray look of a battleship's side and the wind came from the north in sporadic, blustery puffs. Only an occasional scattered rise was visible and the trout were even more reluctant than they had been the week before. I fished slowly and carefully through the afternoon, but still had nothing to show for my efforts by the time I came again to the old cedar with the sagging limb.

Again the chironomids were hatching, but they were fewer this time and there were no rises. There was no sign of life under the limb. Knowing that trout in lakes tend to cruise about and change position rapidly, I had no thought or expectation that the trout I had hooked the week before would still be there. Nonetheless, the dark water under the cedar limb seemed as likely a spot as any other and I decided to try it once again.

This time it was necessary to maneuver to the opposite side of the limb to take advantage of the north breeze. As before, I dropped the fly above the limb and waited while it drifted underneath. Suddenly the fly was gone and there was a single large bubble floating in its place. I raised the rod and a large trout thrashed the surface.

This time, I thought, I've hooked him solidly. But just in the moment it took to think so, the fly came away. I drew it back and examined it; the tiny, fine-wire hook had been straightened by the heavy fish. And I was certain it was the same fish I had hooked the week before.

Another two weeks went by before my next visit to Pass Lake. This time I headed directly for the overhanging limb. But this time someone was there ahead of me, a young man wading along the shoreline, casting a dry fly. I hailed him and we exchanged greetings, and then I asked him whether he had yet cast under the cedar limb.

"Yes," he replied with excitement. "I hooked a big fish that jumped and broke my leader."

I knew then that I would not get another chance at the fish that day, and I was glad somehow that it had kept its freedom.

It was late in the fall before I spent another day on Pass Lake. By then the water level had fallen, and the sagging cedar limb was over dry land. I wondered if the big trout had survived the summer to find another feeding station in the lake, or whether some other angler, luckier or more skilled than I, had found his hiding place and captured him.

I have mentioned this experience because there are two things about it that seemed unusual. One was that it is rare for trout in lakes to remain in the same place, though the extraordinary cover provided by the sagging cedar limb would help to explain it. The other was that it is not often that anglers on the Pacific Slope find a trout so willing to rise consistently to a floating fly—especially in a lake.

Many Western rivers, especially those of the Northwest, are large, fast, brawling streams. They fall rapidly and flood frequently and they are freestone streams with only relatively sparse fly life.

There are notable exceptions, of course, especially on the inland streams—the food-rich Montana rivers, Henry's Fork and Silver Creek in Idaho, Oregon's Deschutes and Williamson, and others. But in many Western rivers, a good, sustained hatch is something of a rarity, and in some of them the primary fishery is for anadromous fish that do not come into the rivers to feed.

That is why so much trout fishing is done on lakes in the Western states and provinces. But even in the richest lakes, there is so much subsurface food that a really good rise to flies on the surface comes only infrequently. Again, there are exceptions—the great mayfly and sedge hatches on Oregon's Hosmer Lake, the mayfly on Davis Lake in the same state, the sedge hatches on the better lakes of the British Columbia interior. But more often than not, the trout will be feeding below the surface on freshwater shrimp or the nymphs and pupae of aquatic insects, and sometimes they range deep and feed mostly on snails.

Still, there are occasions—such as the one on Pass Lake—when rises come often enough to make the dry fly worthwhile. But it is not dry-fly fishing in the classic sense because the angler does not have to cope with currents and eddies and drag.

As a beginning angler, I used the dry fly often. And surprisingly, I caught many trout at first. In particular I remember a sunny April day when I came upon a heavy mayfly hatch in the shallows of Bay Lake, near Tacoma.

It was a windy day and the flies were hatching thickly over the weedbeds, with big rainbow trout rising to them eagerly. It was an afternoon of furious excitement and I ended it with one trout over three pounds and several over two, and I began to wonder why more anglers did not use the dry fly.

Further experience taught me why: In Western fishing, the wet fly and nymph are effective far more often than the dry fly. Looking back over the journals I have kept throughout the years, I see now that I have used dry flies only 10 to 20 percent of the time. And even that, I suspect, is more often than most anglers who fish the majority of their time on Northwest streams and lakes.

The literature of angling is filled with many great works of entomology, most of them dealing with the mayfly, and whole schools of angling tactics and fly dressing have grown up around the imitation of this single insect family. Dry-fly tactics based on imitation of the mayfly flowered in England under the development of Halford and Marryat, and Theodore Gordon revamped their thinking to suit the requirements of America's Catskill streams. Gordon's work was further developed by Hewitt, LaBranche and Jennings, and more recently by Marinaro, Schwiebert and Flick. Their books constitute the backbone of dry-fly theory and practice in America.

But for all the years spent in the development of this knowledge, it remains largely irrelevant in the West. Perhaps it is because of the great variety of fish and insect species and conditions present on Western waters that a coherent "Western school" of angling theory has yet to be devised.

Or perhaps it is because the sport is still developing in the West, and the bold thinkers and innovators who will write the definitive treatises on Western angling have yet to arrive on the scene.

In any case, it is clear that there are vast differences between the traditional approaches employed on Eastern waters with their surface and terrestrial hatches, and the tactics used on the broad, swift rivers and windblown lakes of the West.

Several years ago, an Eastern firm that was compiling data for a calendar of hatches wrote the game department in my state seeking information on local emergences, and the department sent the letter on to me in hopes that I could answer it. I suspect the authors of the calendar were a little surprised at my reply that we did not have any hatches worth cataloging. There has been little research on Western hatches, and their relative sparsity discourages anyone who might set out to do the job.

But good hatches sometimes do occur, even on the majority of waters that are not known for them. Mostly they are of short duration, and always they are unpredictable because of the rapidly changing conditions present on most waters. And sometimes they take place where the angler least expects to find them.

One day I waded up a small tributary of a major river, hoping to find cutthroat that had come in early from the sea. At one time the creek had carried a substantial flow of water through the year, winding down from the hills through a thick forest that kept the water cool and clear. But then loggers had attacked the upper watershed and raped it (there is no better word), and now the stream pours in a thick, brown flood through the spring runoff and then subsides quickly to a trickle of water, naked and open to the sun. And so it was on this day, when only a small stream of water—hardly enough to flow over the feet of my waders—spilled its way down through the piles of shattered gravel heaped up earlier by the floods. I had not seen the stream since it had been devastated, and I quickly lost any hope of finding fish within its reaches, or of seeing any insect life.

But I was wrong on both counts. A hatch began over the shallow riffles, with dozens of tiny mayflies riding down the weakened current and then taking to the air. Soon there were hundreds of them, and then still more, until everywhere I looked the air was filled with the motion of gossamer insects in gentle flight. It seemed impossible that such a hatch could occur in a stream that had been so sadly abused, but there it was. Still, there were no trout to rise to the hatching flies. There was no cover for them in the sun-drenched shallows of the little stream.

But then, on the way back, I explored a side channel carved by the spring floods and found a place where a small spring bubbled out of the ground and flowed in above a great old stump. The springwater had worn a large, deep hole under the stump, and ferns growing on the stump itself kept the water shaded from the sun. I watched the hole, looking for a rise, but there was none, and finally I made a short roll cast and let the gentle current carry a small nymph down to the spot, where an eddy sucked it out of sight. I felt a sudden pull and struck back, and there was a flash of gold as a large cutthroat came tumbling out from under the stump. It ran strongly downstream, where a strand of barbed wire from an old fence sagged into the water, and quickly took my leader around the wire. It left me the fly and the task of untangling the leader.

Good hatches—and good rises—occur so haphazardly on Western waters that I never go out with the expectation of finding them. But they happen just often enough that I always go prepared to deal with them if they should occur. And on those rare occasions when everything goes just right—when the new flies are thick on the water, and the trout come eagerly and fast to naturals and imitations alike—it provides a sense of satisfaction that one seldom receives from using the wet fly or the nymph. Perhaps that is why good hatches on Western waters are so often discussed, so well remembered and so much appreciated.

# A Day
## on the Yuba

Each year in the spring, the shad seek out the fog-shrouded entrance of the Golden Gate and pass quickly through it to the filth and traffic of San Francisco Bay. In unnumbered thousands they find they way through the silt and shifting currents of the great bay to the muddy mouth of the Sacramento River.

Still unseen, the silver hordes enter the river and pass upstream beyond the busy docks and the freeway bridges, swimming up against the river's broad flow and into the hot, dry-grass country of the Sacramento Valley. And there they seek the mouths of their native tributaries—the Feather, the Yuba and the American.

Far to the north, another great run comes back to the Columbia, crossing the great, stormswept bar at the river's mouth. They struggle upstream past the Portland waterfront, dividing at the entrance of Camas Slough where thousands turn aside to spawn at the Washougal River's mouth. The remainder of the run continues up the main stem until it is caught in the violence of the Bonneville tailrace, and there the fish mill in confusion until they find the gentler flow of the fish ladders at the dam. The shad ascend the ladders and disappear on their way to still undiscovered spawning grounds in the upper Columbia and the Snake.

The shad is not native to the West. It was brought from its native Eastern rivers and stocked in the Sacramento and the Columbia in the 1870s. In the hundred years since, the runs have built themselves to major proportions, spilling over into other rivers as they did so.

The shad is a member of the herring family, and it looks very much like a giant herring. It has a large, tender mouth and heavy gill rakers used to trap the plankton that is its primary food during its years at sea. When the shad matures and returns to its native river to spawn, its dime-sized scales are silver-bright and gleam with a mother-of-pearl luster in the sun. Shad are streamlined, deep-bodied fish, and when hooked their favorite maneuver is to turn their broad sides against the current and use its leverage against the angler.

Female shad grow larger than males. The average is three to four pounds, but individuals of seven or eight pounds have been caught. The shad runs well and jumps well, and though its fight pales in comparison to that of a fresh-run steelhead, it still is a strong, lively, fly-rod fish.

In California, the anglers flock to the Sacramento tributaries when the shad are in, and the shad fishery has become an important one. Yet, strangely, anglers have been slow to take advantage of the big Columbia River run. A few fishermen who have discovered the sporting qualities of shad journey faithfully to the Washougal's mouth or the Bonneville tailwaters to fish for them, but the great majority of the Columbia River shad never see an angler's lure.

Perhaps one reason is that the fishing is difficult and the surroundings far from pleasing. The Columbia is far too large and dangerous to wade at Camas and at Bonneville. At Camas, a boat is necessary to reach the main schools of fish, and anglers must hazard the obnoxious fumes from a huge pulp mill. Sometimes the air becomes so foul it is difficult to breathe and nearly impossible to see the far bank of the river. Even when the wind carries the fumes away, the landscape is ugly with clusters of high-tension power poles and heaps of refuse from the mill.

At Bonneville, the river is too swift for any but the largest, strongest boats, and anglers who try to fish from shore confront a steep, stone bank that leaves little room for backcasts. To make matters more difficult, the prevailing wind sweeps in against the shore and limits the range of even the finest casters.

The scenery along the Sacramento tributaries is not much better: flat, dry fields and scrub willows along the riverbanks, with little shade from the sun. But here at least the angler can wade the cool, shallow rivers and often see his quarry before he casts.

The Yuba River is especially popular, and anglers from all over California and beyond gather there each Memorial Day to catch the shad spawning run at its peak.

Memorial Day was just past and so was the peak of the run when I made my first visit to the Yuba. Still, the fish were there in great numbers, and so were the fishermen.

Bill McGrath and I rendezvoused in the dawn and set out in his car for the long drive out of the traffic-clogged Bay Area suburbs, north through onion-scented Vacaville and into the open spaces and smaller towns of the Sacramento Valley. Bill had fished the Yuba many times and knew the route well.

East of Marysville we turned off the highway onto a rutted dirt road that led down to the river, flushing huge jackrabbits from the high grass as we passed. Where we came to the river it was surrounded by high banks of gravel, dredged and sifted and dredged again by generations of gold seekers until literally every stone along the river had been prodded and poked, examined and re-examined. A bewildering array of high-tension lines crossed the river at half a dozen points with no apparent coherence to their patterns, and jet aircraft rumbled and throbbed overhead on the approach to a nearby air base.

We parked among the gravel mounds, put up our rods and walked down to the river. It was midmorning and warm, but a strong wind was blowing up the river between the twin walls of rubble left by the gold dredges. The drift that Bill had chosen for us to fish already was crowded with anglers, most of them fly fishermen, and they told us the fishing had been slow.

We waded out onto the smooth, gently sloping gravel of the river bottom and began casting toward the far bank where the water was faster and deeper.

I was using a fast-sinking fly line, standard equipment for the big, swift water of the Columbia, but the Yuba was low and some of the other anglers were fishing with floating lines—the first time I had seen them used for shad. As I watched one of the other casters, there was a quick swirl behind his line; he struck, and was fast to a shad.

Moments later I heard a shout from Bill and turned to see his rod bent in a tight arc. His reel buzzed as the fish took line, but he recovered it quickly, and after a spirited struggle he eased the fish into the shallows and discovered that his fly had foul-hooked the shad in its head. Bill twisted the fly free and returned the fish to the river.

After that there was little action for a long while, and the crowd along the drift began to thin as anglers left for other parts of the river. We moved upstream to what appeared to be more desirable water, a fast run breaking down over a rocky chute and fanning out into a deeper drift below.

The wind had subsided to an occasional, gentle gust that rattled the scrub-willow leaves. The sun was tall in the sky and hot, and scattered, chiming birds competed with the grumble and whine of insects and the slow, sullen sound of the river. Here and there crows picked at the rotting remains of spawned-out shad, and a big blue heron flew along the crest of a mountain of gold tailings. I cast into the faster water and let the current take the fly in a sweeping semicircle until the long line was straight below me.

Then came the sudden, jolting strike so characteristic of a shad, and the heavy Beaudex reel sang a baritone growl that rose quickly to a tenor's pitch. The shad took a long length of line downstream, then veered quickly toward the bank and took the line right around the feet of another angler.

The other fisherman sensed the strange pressure on his waders and glanced down to see the cause of it. He saw the line through the clear water and stepped back so that it came free and once again was taut to the fish.

Thwarted there, the shad turned back into the current, shifting and turning its broad body to take full advantage of the faster water. Then it jumped in the peculiar way shad have of jumping, coming out in a flat trajectory, coming down to slap the water with its side.

Slowly the fish tired and I recovered the line it had taken. And finally it was resting on the gravel at my feet, a bright female gleaming in the sun. The fly came easily from the soft jaw and I eased the fish gently back into the river, holding it erect until its strength returned.

Now there was a flurry of activity. Quickly I landed two other fish and lost a third. Bill hooked another and had a hard fight with it in the fast water, discovering when he landed it that it, too, had been foul-hooked. But then the flurry subsided as quickly as it had come. We fished on for a while, then drove into Marysville to eat lunch and browse through the tackle shops.

In the afternoon we returned to the river, at a point farther downstream. We fished there an hour, seeing no fish and hooking none. It was late in the day when we returned to Bill's car and headed upriver again, stopping this time just below a small irrigation dam. The water slid smoothly over the round face of the dam and broke into a large, oblong pool at the bottom. It moved in curious, indecisive eddies through the pool, then gathered itself together and spilled down a narrow, shallow chute to the head of a second, smaller pool below. It was the second pool we chose to fish.

I waded deep into the upstream end of the pool and cast out and down, watching the line swing and sink in the current. The sun was low in the sky, with fierce light glinting obliquely off the moving surface of the pool, but I could make out the massive, ghostly shapes of boulders rearing up beneath the water. I thought to myself that it would make fine holding water for steelhead, and looking deep into the pool I conjured up a mental image of the shadowy form of a fresh summer-run steelhead swaying in a gentle eddy behind a boulder.

And then the image moved.

The light had shifted just a little, just enough to show that what I had thought was only a figment of imagination was in reality a fish. And it was quickly joined by another, and then another, and suddenly it seemed as if a thousand silver leaves were drifting through the pool, turning slowly in the current, glinting with dull flashes as the light caught their shifting sides. But they were not steelhead, nor were they leaves—they were shad!

A great school of fish was in the pool, and as I watched it

slowly circled, moving first to the head of the pool where the fast water flowed into it, then turning back and passing out of sight on the far side, only to reappear at the foot of the pool and begin the circuit once again.

I watched the progress of the school and cast so that the current would sweep my fly into the head of it as it came around again. Suddenly there came a solid strike, and a shad leaped near the foot of the pool. It made the characteristic run, then turned and came back, and I fought it in close until only the leader showed beyond my rod tip. The fish was turning and fighting right in the center of the school, now so close that shad were nearly brushing against my waders, but the other fish paid no attention to the struggles of their brother. I backed out of the pool onto the high, rocky bank and eased the fish ashore. After releasing it, I waded out and cast again, and soon another fish came, and then another, and the action grew even faster as the light dwindled and evening came on.

Bill, fishing just upstream, had several strikes, but could not seem to get a solid hook-up. Then, moving to a new spot, he slipped on a rock and sat down hard in the river. He emerged, dripping and profane, and headed back to his car to change clothes. I stayed on, fishing until the last light drained out of the day and mosquitoes came out of the brush to settle eagerly on my hands and face.

Finally I released a last fish and climbed back over the gravel bank to where Bill was waiting in the car. It had not been one of Bill's better days, but soon he would get another chance at the river. For me, it had been a pleasant and unusual change from fishing in the ugly, roaring violence of the Columbia, a chance to wade a small river and to see what I was fishing for.

I found myself wishing that the Columbia offered similar sport. Perhaps one day it will, if more Northwest anglers begin to fish for shad and ferret out the upstream spawning grounds, and if nitrogen poisoning does not kill the shad as it has most of the native salmon and steelhead of the Columbia.

And if the Columbia does not develop such sport, then perhaps it will come later in some other, smaller river, where even now the shad may be building up a run that so far has escaped the attention of anglers. And even if it never comes at all, it is not really so very far to the Yuba and her sister rivers—where men once searched for gold and anglers now search happily for silver.

# After Dark

James Chetham, writing in *The Angler's Vade Mecum* (1681), called night fishing an "unwholesome, unpleasant and very ungenteel" sport, and a practice "to be used by none but idle poaching fellows."

Without doubt there is more than a grain of truth in what he says, and certainly the literature of angling is replete with tales of poachers and perpetrators of other foul angling deeds who committed their crimes under cover of darkness.

But if it is true that the darkest hours bring out the worst in men, it also is true that they bring out the best of trout. Great trout, quiescent by day, begin to prowl and feed at night, and hidden hatches set off explosive rises from fish the daytime angler never sees. For those anglers whose intentions are honorable and above reproach, the hours of darkness may provide angling of an exciting, different sort.

I am not a night fisherman by regular habit, but occasionally when the day is warm and the wind gentle I will stay on the water long after the last light fades, and try to tempt the larger trout that come forth to feed at night. And occasionally, when I become aware of the presence of a large trout that will not take my fly by day, I make a special trip to try for him by night. More often than not these expeditions are successful, but successful or not they never fail to generate high excitement.

Night angling has a special quality. As the last light steals from the day, the earth changes suddenly in a confusing movement of dark and growing shadows. Familiar landmarks grow or shrink, become magnified in total size as individual details disappear, or dwindle into obscure and hidden shadows. A well-known place becomes suddenly mysterious and strange, forbidding and forbidden, and as total darkness descends all reference points slowly disappear until only the tops of the tallest ridges remain silhouetted dimly against the sky.

The stars begin their slow, silent climb to the zenith, and perhaps there is a pale moon with light enough to cast cold, silver shadows across the meadows or the mesas. The familiar life of day is gone and the creatures of the night take over. The rings from rising fish gleam briefly like spreading circles of molten steel in the ghostly evening light, and the swallows that fed on the daylight hatches are replaced by silent, plunging bats.

The night fisherman knows a different world. Normal daytime sounds subside so that one may hear the soft, close rush of wings from a bird in hidden flight. The bullfrogs talk to one another more freely than by day, and the loud slap of a beaver's tail echoes through the wild. The moon trades its cold light with the clouds, and occasionally meteors flash overhead with a last quick burst of dying flame. The stars wheel in their silent orbits—bright Rigel and mysterious Betelgeuse, and the Arab mourners plodding eternally after a casket traced in stars.

It is a time to pause, to look up in awe and wonder about the nature of things; a time that teaches humility in the face of evidence that the angler is only a small fisherman on a small water, an infinitesimal fragment of life hurtling through the void from an unknown source to an uncharted destination, with only his fragile faith to guide him.

But if it is a time for contemplation, it also is a time for action. There comes the sudden sound of a heavy rise, and the angler wheels blindly toward the sound and casts into the night. His fly rides an invisible wave and tensely he waits for the sound of a take or the sudden jolt that will tell him the trout has seen what he cannot see.

And then follows the struggle with an invisible opponent, a silent battle between a man who cannot see his quarry and a trout robbed of the sanctuary of familiar obstacles now hidden in the dark. And when it is over the angler is either flushed and trembling with the excitement of victory or filled with the pangs of defeat and wonder at the size of the unseen thing that defeated him.

My first real try at night fishing came on a warm September evening in central British Columbia. We were camped in the bottom of a great granite canyon with ancient Indian pictographs painted on its walls. The canyon held a pair of lakes, twin jewels of sparkling clear water with shallow, sandy shoals that sloped off into unknown turquoise depths.

I had spent the day fishing one of them, and in the shallow water behind a large weedbed I had found trout rising freely to a hatch. I had taken and released many on a dry fly, but most of them were small and I was frustrated because I could see much larger fish moving in and out of the shallows to feed. The larger fish refused everything I tried, wet fly, or dry, and so I waited to fish the evening rise in hopes they would be less cautious then.

The light went quickly off the water in the deep canyon, and the sky changed from blue to deep purple. But there was no hatch and no rise, and I watched and waited as the last light disappeared without seeing a single ring on the placid surface of the lake. The next day we would have to leave and return to the city, and I badly wanted at least one more good fish before we left, so I determined to wait even until after total darkness had fallen. I had with me a small flashlight to aid in changing flies or leaders, and I settled down to wait.

It was quiet in the darkness, except for a gentle stir of breeze that set the tules rubbing against one another and pushed small wavelets at my boat that made a tiny lap-lap sound as they struck its windward side. And then, far back in the weeds, came the heavy splash of a feeding trout. It was far beyond casting range, and hopelessly hidden in the weeds, and so I waited further. Far off came the sound of another splashing rise and I sensed rather than saw the great, mothlike sedges that were beginning to flutter awkwardly from the surface of the lake.

Another heavy splash, this one close by, just at the edge of the weedbed from the sound of it. I cast quickly toward the sound, and as I felt the line strike the water in the darkness there was another explosive rise, and I struck instinctively. There was immediate, furious resistance from a fish so strong I thought for a moment I could not hold it on the light tackle. It ran along the edge of the weedbed and my reel screamed in angry protest. I felt the backing splice slide out through the guides and heard a great crash in the darkness as the fish leaped and fell back into the water.

Then it was a long and silent struggle as the fish turned and plunged and vainly sought the sanctuaries it used by day.

It was confused in the darkness and turned away from the weedbed where it would have broken me off quickly, and I held it as firmly as I could so that it would not stray again out of the deeper water into which it had blundered.

Time passes quickly in the darkness, and it seemed a very long time indeed before all the line was back on the reel and only the leader extended beyond the tip of the rod. The trout circled the boat once, then again, and in the starlight I caught a glimpse of silver and stabbed at it with the net. The surface erupted as the net closed around the trout and I lifted it clear, struggling and twisting in the mesh. And then it lay quivering in the bottom of my boat, illuminated by the wavering beam of my flashlight, a great old trout of many summers, with broad silver flanks that bounced the light back into my eyes.

It had been as exciting a fight as I had ever had with a fish, and though I had waited for darkness with some reservations about the ethics of it all, I felt now that no trout ever had been more honestly taken or had struggled more nobly than this one. And as for the ethics of the matter, if the trout was somewhat handicapped by the darkness, the angler had been handicapped even more, and is not the taking of fish under difficult circumstances indeed the essence of the sport?

For me, the answer was affirmative, and with that question having been resolved my path has led to other nighttime waters.

I suspect all anglers are night fishermen in their hearts. Who among us has ever fished who did not look forward to the evening, the long, drawn-out death of the day when, as every angler knows, the trout grow less cautious and the fishing more rewarding? When does evening end and night begin? What is less honorable about fishing when the darkness is nearly total than fishing when a little light remains? What separates the night fisherman from the man who stays to fish the "evening rise"?

It is, of course, a matter of definition, and each angler has his own idea of the best time to fish and the best time to quit fishing, whether it be at five o'clock or midnight. Perhaps the most eloquent answer was that given by the great angling pioneer Thaddeus Norris, who said:

"Of all places, commend me, in the still of the evening, to the long placid pool, shallow on one side, with deeper water and an abrupt overhanging bank opposite. Where the sun has shone all day, and legions of ephemera sported in its declining rays; the bloom of the rye or clover scenting the air from the adjoining field! Now light a fresh pipe, and put on a pale Ginger Hackle for your tail-fly, and a little white-winged Coachman for your dropper. Then wade in cautiously—move like a shadow—don't make a ripple. Cast, slowly, long, light; let your stretcher sink a little. There, he has taken the Ginger—lead him around gently to the shallow side as you reel him in, but don't move from your position—let him tug awhile, put your net under him, break his neck, and slip him into your creel. Draw your line through the rings—cast again; another and another—keep on until you can see only the ripple made by your fly; or know when it falls, by the slight tremor it imparts through the whole line down to your hand— until the whippoorwill beings his evening song, and the little frog tweets in the grass close by;—not till then is it time to go home."

And so it is, in the sweet of the evening.

Three springs ago, I spent an evening among the rushes at Dry Falls Lake, at the head of the great coulee where eons ago the Columbia River plunged over in a mighty falls many times the height and width of Niagara. Now there is nothing left but the huge, silent, eroding walls of stone, and the rich lake that fills the old catchbasin where once the river fell.

It had been a bright, hot day, with the temperature well up in the 80s and the sun peering brightly into the depths. The fishing had been poor, as it usually is under such circumstances, and now I was waiting for the light to die beyond the coulee rim.

The light was a long time fading from the water, but slowly it did so and the great rocks reached out with shadows to replace the brilliance of the day. And as the shadows deepened, the trout began to move into the shallows to feed, with a steady march of rises to the shore.

I cast toward the rises and strained in the gathering darkness to see my fly. It was hopeless; my eyes were not keen enough to pick out the tiny dark pattern and separate it from the dark water on which it rode. So, holding the fine point of the leader up to the twilight in order to see what I was about, I tied on a larger pattern with hackle fore-and-aft and cast it out. This one I could see, with its dark bulk riding on stiff hackles as it waited for a trout to notice it was there.

I teased the fly with my rod tip so that it crept across the surface, and quickly it was gone, swallowed up in a rising wave by a trout which had it and was quickly away. There was no need to lift the rod; the tension came immediately as the fish began a powerful run. My reel on this occasion was an especially noisy one, and the echo of its ratchet rattled off the coulee walls as the trout took all the line and the backing quickly followed. He jumped, sixty yards out, and when I thought of the fine, 6X tippet on the leader, I had no hope that I would ever have him.

The trout turned and came back a little way, and once again I had some line on the reel. But then it was off again on another run, this one perpendicular to the first, and took the line around a clump of tules growing in the shallows. I slacked off to keep tension from the line and avoid a break in the leader.

For a long moment, nothing happened, and I stood there holding slack line. And then I saw the tip of my floating white line in the faint light beyond the tules, moving slowly through the shadows. The trout was still on. There was only one way I would ever get him out of the spot where he had gone, and risky as it was I had to try it. I threw a great loop in the line, almost as if I were mending an upstream cast. The loop cleared the tops of the tules and fell in open water on the other side. I reeled in, tightened, and once again felt the resistance of the fish.

From then on it was a long, slow, delicate fight, the trout tired from its two long runs and I afraid to be heavy-handed because of the light leader tripper. Finally the trout was kicking feebly in the shallows and I had my net under it. It was a rainbow, one of the prettiest I have seen, clean and bright with a sharp dividing line between the silver of its sides and the gunmetal gray of its back. I removed the hook from the gristle of its jaw and eased it back into the water, holding it for a long time until it regained strength enough to swim slowly away.

It was pitch dark when I started back, and I heard the faint call of the vanguard of a flock of Canada geese, winging their way north after a winter spent on the flats of Tulelake in California's northern hills, or in the grain-rich fields of the Sacramento Valley. Soon the flock was directly overhead, and though the great birds were invisible against the night, their haunting calls filled the great stone amphitheater with sound, echoing and re-echoing long after the flock itself had passed. It had been a satisfying day, rich with sensations of sight and sound and feel.

I have spent nights on many waters, gazing up at the Southern Cross while the gentle trade wind rippled at my shirt, or watching the silent flicker of the Northern Lights play across the horizon of a Canadian lake. I have fought a losing match with a great brown trout that took my fly on the darkest of all nights, and a winning contest with a giant rainbow that fell upon my fly in the middle of a night hatch where hordes of insects swayed and brushed lightly against my face and hands, all unseen. I have thrilled to the cry of a cougar and the lost, lonely call of a loon, the wildest sound in all of nature; and I have fought silent battles with unseen trout while coyotes howled in the hills.

The night is not to be feared; it is to be felt, touched, sampled and explored. It is filled with exciting secrets forever hidden from the day. It is a frontier, to be tried and tested and won, and I commend it to all anglers.

# Spring
## in British Columbia

Once I made to myself a vow that I would never again fish in British Columbia in the spring. So many spring trips had been miserable, with freezing cold and snow at night, hard rain and sleet by day, with vicious muddy roads and fishing that was terrible at least as often as it was good.

But of course I made the vow at the end of a trip during which the weather had been particularly mean, and I forgot it almost as quickly as it was made. And now at least once each spring I head north into the interior, fully aware that my chances for success hinge on the fickle vagaries of weather, but also aware that some of my most pleasant memories have come from these spring expeditions.

There was, for instance, the year when we arrived at Hihium Lake on the 15th of May, the first anglers to visit the lake that year. Four inches of snow had fallen the night before our arrival, and at night it was so cold that we bundled up in heavy clothing and slept as close to the big wood stove as we could get. The days were cold, too, but the trout were eager and hungry and rose willingly to the first chironomid hatches, and we caught them by the dozen on dry flies.

There was a warm, bright spring afternoon when I drove to a small lake near Merritt and launched my boat. I had never fished it so early in the season and the lake was far higher than I had ever seen it.

But everything else about it was familiar; the thick stand of timber growing down to its southern shore, the waving green fields of grass stretching away to the north. A pair of stately loons glided on its clear water and an equally handsome pair of ospreys looked down from a tall pine. A badger scampered along the bank and disappeared in the timber, and a gentle breeze sent wavelets sliding in against the rocky beach. I felt a warm, happy feeling such as one has when greeting an old, dear friend after a long absence.

I rowed out into the lake, empty except for me, and anchored in a favorite spot. I stood up in the boat and stripped line from the reel for the first cast, and even as I did so I saw a fish dimple cautiously close by. I cast toward the spot and dropped the little shrimp fly where the rise had been, then began the slow, deliberate retrieve. Suddenly there was a vicious strike and a great trout shot straight upward, its bright sides flashing in the sun. The trout was off and running hard, and a sudden gust of wind dislodged my anchor and sent the boar drifting out into deep water, making it that much more difficult to cope with the determined trout. The little Hardy reel screamed until I feared for its bearings, and the trout seemed to be all over the lake at once, jumping, tail-walking, twisting, shaking and wrapping itself in the leader. It was a long struggle, made more difficult by the gusting wind and the drifting boat, but at last I led the trout alongside, thrust the net under it, and lifted it—dripping and squirming—into the boat. There I quickly weighed and measured it—twenty-four inches and six and a half pounds—and then gently slipped it back into the lake.

And that was only the start. In the hours before darkness, I took two other fish, nearly as large, and lost three others that broke water in silver bursts in the gathering dusk and then shook themselves free. Every pine on the far hill was traced in vivid silhouette against a sky of dark flame when I left the lake, deeply satisfied with the day, and a solitary coyote barked a greeting to a rising full moon as I took my leave.

But those were pleasant times. There was also the time on the road to Derry Lake when the Jeep skidded on a rock in the middle of a bottomless gumbo mudhole and became stuck so deeply that water was running in through the tailgate. I shoveled and jacked and pushed and strained for half an hour trying to free it, but gained not a single inch. Then another fisherman came along in a pickup truck and, in trying to pull me out, got himself stuck too. But he had a hand winch which he used to pull himself free and which we then used to free the Jeep. A crust of dried gumbo covered me from head to foot, and my respect for this peculiarly thick, viscous type of mud grew another notch.

On one trip I quickly became convinced that a storm had become attached to me and was bound to follow wherever I went—a fate similar to that of the unfortunate character in Al Capp's comic strip who was born with a black cloud over his head that follows and rains on him wherever he goes.

His was a small cloud compared to mine, however—mine was a towering collection of clouds that stretched darkly from one horizon to the other and reached out occasionally with bright bolts of lightning and freezing rain and sleet, followed sometimes by bursts of wet snow. And though I went to half a dozen widely scattered lakes, it followed me to every one, and lashed the surfaces of them all with high winds and rain and hail.

I worked my way west and finally stopped at Tunkwa Lake, but the storm was only a couple of hours behind me. No sooner had I begun fishing than the first telltale gust of wind stirred the surface and the familiar dark thunderheads rolled in across the pinetops and exploded in violence. Fierce blue lightning flashes reached into the forest, followed by a roll of thunder like all the cannons of history firing together. The waves quickly built themselves into whitecaps, splashing up over the sides of the boat and spilling water into it, and then—almost before I could struggle into my rain gear—the rain came, a thick gray veil sweeping down the hills, heralding its approach with a few large, spattering drops. And then it was upon the lake with a dull roar of water, a great, drenching sheet of drops, and I began the long row back into the teeth of the wind.

Reaching shore, I quickly packed my gear and headed down the road to Six Mile Lake. It was at a much lower elevation and I thought perhaps it would escape the storm.

The sky was dark and unpromising when I arrived, but the surface of the lake was calm and here and there were the rings of trout rising to a hatch. I quickly launched and rowed out among them. They proved to be discerning trout and it took some experimentation to find a pattern they would take. But soon I found one that did the job, and in a moment I was playing my first fish. I landed it and released it, then stood up to make another cast. The air was quiet and still, and then there came a distant cannonroll of thunder and scattered drops of rain hit the surface around me. Little williwaws of wind suddenly chased themselves across the surface, stirring dark riffles that collided with one another. One of them spun my boat around and threw a belly into the floating line, and before I could retrieve it the storm struck with all its strength. The forest moaned as a hundred thousand pines bent before an invisible wall of wind, and the scattered drops of rain turned into a stinging fusillade of hail. Lightning spat from the dark sky and dirty whitecaps raced across the lake, and I was drenched and shivering before I could get into my still-wet poncho.

That was the last straw, and I decided it was time to head for home. The storm raged all around as I hauled the boat up through the mud and loaded it onto the truck, quickly changed into some dry clothes and started to drive out, with the truck's windshield wipers trying vainly to clear away the wall of mixed rain, snow and sleet that now was falling.

Lightning strikes straddled the road and the truck shook from the concussion of thunder as I started alone from the lake. I had gone a mile and had driven to the top of a steep rise when suddenly I came upon a sight that made me stop in awe.

All around the pine forest was hidden in dark, shifting waves of rain and hail, broken momentarily by splintered lines of lightning, but in front of me a shaft of deep golden afternoon light poured through an opening in the clouds and illuminated a brillilant green meadow in the pines, and beyond it was a rainbow so vivid that the colors hurt the eye. I got out of the truck and stood in the moisture-laden air, heavy with ozone, while the earth trembled from the thunder and the lightning cast weird, split-second shadows, and gazed on the splendid sight, so perfect in its beauty it seemed as if the very gates of heaven had opened before my eyes. When I think of the interior country, a land that I love deeply, I think of that sight.

Spring fishing in the British Columbia interior can change at a moment's notice. I remember another day on Tunkwa Lake when an incredible hatch of chironomids was in progress. The insects came off the water by the thousands, in all sizes, and each puff of wind blew them like sleet into the faces of the anglers. They were in our ears and eyes and their empty cases were so numerous that they floated in windrows on the surface and hung, two or three at a time, from each leader knot at the end of every retrieve.

For days the trout had gorged themselves on the great hatch and would take nothing. For nine long hours I fished, without a single strike, trying every chironomid imitation I had and fishing in every reasonable way I could think of. But then, in the last hour of the day, the rise began, with big fish cruising in a steady line across the mouth of a shallow bay. And in that brief, exciting hour before final darkness, I hooked ten fish, and the long, fruitless hours of the day were soon forgotten.

Each spring, when the Americans celebrate Memorial Day, the fly-fishing clubs of the Northwest gather at Peter-hope Lake in British Columbia to compete for the Totem Trophy. The trophy consists of a reel and a line dryer once owned by the late angling artist Tommy Brayshaw, whose name still is deeply revered by Northwest anglers. The reel and dryer, polished to a fine glow, are handsomely mounted in a glass case with brass plates engraved with the names of the winning clubs. While winning the trophy is considered an honor, the competition is second to the fellowship that ensues when anglers gather to renew friendships that transcend state lines and international borders. At night the lakeside flickers with campfires and the sound of bagpipes and song, and many a tall tale and angling secret is passed back and forth over the flaming embers in the spring night. The fishing never seems particularly good at that time, and perhaps that in itself is good because it makes the contest a more truthful test of angling skill.

When the contest is over and the trophy has been awarded to the winning club for the coming year, the anglers quickly break camp and head for home or for other fishing waters. And so it was one year that when the festivities were done I elected to set out for nearby Blue Lake, which I had heard described as a beautiful lake containing some very large trout.

Phil Aigner had been there the day before, and I asked him for directions to find my way through the maze of logging roads that run near the lake.

"It's easy to find," he said. "Just take the main logging road to the Mile 11 sign, then take the left-hand fork to the lake."

Easy enough, I thought, and so I took the main logging road and sure enough, right at the Mile 11 sign the road forked. I took the left-hand fork and began to look around for the lake. Phil had said it was about five miles beyond Peterhope, but the odometer on my truck soon showed that I had gone more than seven miles, and there was no sign of any lake. In addition, the road was getting worse, with some bad mudholes. I was getting a long way from anyone, and I was getting worried. Finally the road became a pair of deep, soft ruts, disappearing here and there into a quagmire of mud, and I had some bad moments as the truck slewed around while I gunned it through the mudholes. I had nearly decided to turn around and go back when the road came to an end. Driving back through the muck, I came again to the Mile 11 sign and got out to see if I could find where I had gone wrong.

And then I discovered that Phil had neglected to tell me there were *two* left-hand forks, and I had driven past the one I should have taken.

I started down the other fork, confident I would soon be at Blue Lake. But before I had driven a hundred yards I heard a whistle and a shout. Back behind me on a side road was a four-wheel-drive truck, stuck deeply in a gumbo mudhole. I recognized the driver as Pete Caverhill, a fisherman from Vancouver whom I had met several times before.

Pete explained that he also had been looking for Blue

Lake and had taken a wrong turn. The road suddenly had given way under his heavy truck and camper, which now was stuck hopelessly. Pete's wife had gone ahead on foot, hoping to find someone at the lake who could help.

I had a small hand winch or "come-along" in my truck, but I told Pete I doubted it had sufficient strength to pull his heavy truck. But I also had a long length of cable, and I offered to try to tow him out with my truck. We looked over the road, and then Pete said, "I don't think you should try. I'm afraid you'll bugger up your own truck."

We stood there a moment, discussing various things we might do to free his truck, when we heard the sound of another truck back on the main road. We yelled and waved and the truck stopped. It was an old pickup, filled with Indians. There were at least eight of them, maybe ten, ranging in age from twelve or fourteen up to fifty or so. One of the older Indians seemed to be the leader, a thick, muscled man with iron-gray hair and a face lined by a life in the sun.

The Indians swarmed around Pete's truck and immediately assumed control of the situation as if they had been rehearsing for just such an occasion. From the back of their pickup they produced a tow chain and hooked one end to Pete's truck and the other to their pickup. Then, with one of the Indians at the wheel of the pickup and Pete in the driver's seat of his own truck, the rest of us got behind the camper and pushed while both drivers applied power. The camper edged forward slowly, its rear wheels spinning wildly in the muck, until it looked as if it would pop free. Then the chain broke.

The leader of the Indians swore. Then he sent the others scurrying over the logged-off landscape until one of them found a discarded piece of timber about twelve feet long. Another hooked my cable to what was left of the broken tow chain. The free end of the cable was made fast around a big stump and the end of the chain was fastened to Pete's truck. Then it became clear that the Indians planned to try to pull the truck out with a "Spanish windlass," an old wilderness trick which I had heard of but never had seen.

The slack part of the chain was doubled around one end of the timber. Then, while Pete urged the engine of his truck, several of the Indians and I walked the timber around in a circle, twisting the chain around it and tightening it link-by-link. As the pressure increased on the chain, it became more and more difficult to turn the timber, and the cable bit deeply into the wood of the stump to which it was fastened. But, little by little, Pete's truck inched forward until once again it looked as if it would come free. Then, once again, the chain broke.

The Indians swore. The sun was hot and all of us were sweating and panting. Mosquitoes came out of the timber and hovered around us in vicious, whining clouds. But the leader of the Indians seemed undismayed. He sent his crew to work with a shovel, and a large hole was dug under the rear of the camper truck. A log was thrown across this, and another timber was placed across the log with the short end under the rear of the camper. Using this as a lever, five or six of us pulled down on the long end, lifting up the back of the camper. The other Indians jammed more timbers underneath, so that for the first time the truck's frame was clear of the mud.

A similar operation was performed on the truck's right rear wheel, which was stuck deepest, and a two-by-six plank from the Indians' pickup was jammed under the tire. Then, with all of us pushing, Pete gunned the engine of his truck. It lurched, the wheels spun and mud flew, and then the truck broke free and drove out onto firm ground. We all sighed in relief and mopped the sweat dripping from our brows.

Pete thanked the Indians and gave them a spare jack in payment for their assistance, and they all piled back into the old pickup and disappeared into the woods.

All this had taken several hours. Now it was late in the day and I was wondering if I would ever get to Blue Lake.

Pete's wife had returned, saying she had not found the lake and that the road ahead had more dangerous mudholes in it.

Pete and I nevertheless decided to try to find the lake together. Because of his wife's warning, we decided to walk ahead to see if the road was passable. Together we walked down a hill and into the welcome shade of the uncut woods, scouting ahead for perhaps a quarter of a mile. There was some mud, but nothing which looked too formidable, and we decided we would try to go ahead. Then, walking back to the place we had left the trucks, we heard a strange noise ahead. An old, incredibly battered Chrysler sedan came into view, bucking and lurching hesitantly over the rough road, and wheezed to a stop in front of us. It was filled with Indian teenagers.

The driver, a lad of eighteen or twenty years, leaped out.

"What's that noise?" he asked. "Is something wrong with my car?"

I looked at the ancient vehicle. It had no front bumper or grille. It was dented and scraped. Several of the windows had spiderweb patterns of broken glass in them. It looked as if it had a lot of things wrong with it.

The car kept edging forward down the hill in six-inch jerks until one of the other passengers jumped out and kicked rocks under the rear wheels.

"We hit something on the way up and broke the brake line," he said. "All the brake fluid ran out, but we filled it up with water and it works pretty good. Except downhill."

Pete and I exchanged glances.

"Why don't you raise the hood and we'll listen to that noise?" I suggested to the driver. He agreed, and one of his companions lifted the hood and held it up with one hand while the driver started the engine and gunned it. There was an explosive rumble and a sound like a washing machine starting up after ten years of inactivity. Blue flame erupted from the rear of the engine.

"Your exhaust manifold is gone," I told the driver. "It's rusted away. That's what's causing the noise."

"Oh, I knew that," he said. "That's not the noise I meant. I mean the funny, high-pitched noise."

We listened a moment and quickly diagnosed the source of the latter noise as a loose fan belt. So loose, in fact, that it wobbled. We showed the driver how to loosen the bolts holding the generator in place and move it until the belt was tight.

"I'll look to see if I have a wrench," the driver said. His friend took away the arm that had been holding up the hood and it fell where our heads had been a moment earlier, landing with a dangerous crash.

The driver untied a length of rubber that was being used to hold the car's trunk shut. He lifted the trunk and looked inside. "I don't have a wrench," he said.

Pete had one in his camper. He went to get it, and the car's hood was propped up with a tree limb so the Indians could work on the generator.

"Where were you guys headed?" Pete asked while they worked.

"Down to the creek at the bottom of the hill," the driver answered. "Goin' to do some fishing."

"Fishing?" Are there fish in the creek?"

"Sure," the Indian said. "Trout. Big ones."

"Are they spawning?"

Suddenly the Indian's face wore a wary look. "Well, yes, I suppose some of them are," he said.

I looked in the back seat of the car. There were three big dip nets and a large burlap bag.

"Don't you know it's illegal to net spawning fish?" Pete asked.

The Indian feigned surprise. "No!" he said. "Really?" It was a masterful performance.

Pete and I assured him that, yes, it really was illegal to

net spawning trout, and furthermore Blue Lake was one of the local game warden's favorite spots (which was true) and that he traveled this road frequently and surely would arrest the driver and his friends if he found them netting spawners from the stream at the bottom of the hill. The Indian nodded solemnly and said that now he and his friends had this knowledge they certainly would not try to net the trout spawning in the stream.

Meanwhile, the Indian working under the hood had stripped the threads on the bolt holding the generator in place so that it was impossible to loosen it.

We told the Indians there was nothing more we could do and they would simply have to make the best of it with a loose fan belt.

The tree limb was removed and the hood fell with another crash. Most of the Indians piled back inside the aged vehicle. Two remained outside; one kicked the rocks out from under the wheels and then both got behind the car and began to push. The car lurched forward down the hill; the engine gurgled, then spluttered into explosive life. The two pushers caught up with the car and jumped in, and with an occasional hiccough the car disappeared into the forest, leaving a heavy scent of burned oil in its wake.

I looked at my wristwatch. It was nearly six o'clock, and I had promised to be back at the Peterhope camp in time for dinner. Still, I decided to go along with Pete and at least have a look at Blue Lake. Pete and his wife planned to spend the night there.

We followed the road for another couple of miles, crossing the creek the Indians had spoken of and spying their car, still filled with its passengers, parked on a spur road waiting for us to pass. And then, finally, shining through the trees was the sparkling surface of Blue Lake.

It was, indeed, a beautiful lake, lying in what appeared to be an old lava vent. Shallow pumice shoals ran around its edge, then disappeared into deep, mysterious depths in the center of the lake. The water was air-clear, and large fish could be seen cruising along the edge of the drop-off.

It would be a challenging place to fish, and under normal circumstances I would have been eager with the anticipation of exploring an untried water. But the exertions of the afternoon had left me tired, and the day was fast drawing to a close. After a few halfhearted casts, I started alone on the return to Peterhope.

The trip back was without incident. But in camp that night, I heard from other fishermen who had come over the same road that a group of young Indians had been seen netting spawning trout from the creek at the bottom of the hill during the time I had been at Blue Lake. I didn't need to ask whether the Indians had been driving a battered old Chrysler.

Such are the adventures one has while fishing in British Columbia in the spring. Sometimes the fishing is slow, and sometimes it is not, but I can't remember a single time when it ever was dull. And I wouldn't miss it for the world.

# Basin Browns

A long search, and there it was—a thin sheet of water glinting through a dip between the hills.

Of course, I still was not certain it was the place I was seeking. My informant had been a little vague, perhaps deliberately so as he realized his indiscretion in giving up what he obviously considered a valuable secret.

Yet if he had been a little uncertain about the location, there was no doubt about the rest of what he had said: "The lake is filled with brown trout, good ones, and they take a dry fly well."

That was enough to stir my interest, because brown trout

are relatively rare in the far Northwest. Their reputation as cannibals, deserved or not, has kept management authorities from planting them where they might get into anadromous rivers and swallow up the fry of steelhead and salmon. A few of them have been stocked here and there in lakes with rainbow trout, but to my knowledge nowhere within five hundred miles was there another lake that held brown trout alone.

And so I had searched through the desert and the dunes of the Columbia Basin until I topped a rise above a large and well-known lake and looked beyond it through that little dip and saw more water. From the map, I could not tell with any certainty whether this was, indeed, the right lake because it was surrounded by numerous other lakes and ponds. But, of course, I would find out.

It was a lonely spot. The fierce wind that blows through the basin came in ugly gusts, kicking up little spirals of sand, carrying them along, discarding them at its whim. It blew choppy riffles across the lake below me and built little waves that shattered themselves against the basalt outcrops.

The surrounding landscape appeared flat, with clumps of sage and bitterbrush and occasional thrusting basalt blocks. But it was not flat; it was crisscrossed with ancient coulees, deep cuts in the earth's surface, some of them so abrupt that one could pass within a few feet of them without knowing they were there. Some of them are filled with water, new lakes created by irrigation drainage; others are dry washes, filled with runoff only when visited by infrequent rains, dry the remainder of the time; and some look as if they had always been dry and always will be.

It is rattlesnake country, and deermouse, jackrabbit, lizard and darkling-beetle country. It also is great bird country—waterfowl and pheasant, hawk and magpie, meadowlark and cliff swallow, yellowhead and redwing blackbird country. And usually it is alive with the myriad songs of its residents, but not today. Even the cattails along the water, a favorite haunt of birds, were silent, bending and bowing in the breeze. A high, thin overcast reduced the sun to a fuzzy patch of light, and there was only the muted thunder of the wind and the rattle of dry bush.

It would be a long hike overland to the little lake beyond the far shore, but it looked to be an easy portage between the two. And so I went back to my truck and steered it gingerly between the rocks, the sandholes and the sage and parked it on a steep bluff overlooking the larger lake. It was difficult getting the cartop boat down the steep bank to the water, and the wind tried to hold me back as I rowed across to the far side. I pulled the boat ashore and hiked about a hundred yards up a gentle, sandy slope and finally stood on the shore of the little lake.

The lake was nestled in a coulee with steeply rising sides in three directions. Only the end from which I had approached was open, and I marveled at how well hidden it was. If I had gone twenty feet in either direction when I was searching I never would have seen its water gleaming through the draw.

Well-sheltered from the wind, the surface of the lake showed only the suggestion of a riffle. I studied it for long moments, hoping for a rise that would indicate it was the lake I was seeking, but there was none. I knelt at the shoreline, turned over a stone and watched freshwater shrimp dart away in confusion. It was a lake obviously rich in aquatic life, shallow, with sweeping weedbeds along the shore. It looked good. If only there were fish in it.

I returned to my boat, pulled up on the shore of the larger lake, and carried it up the gentle rise to the smaller one. There I put up my rod and bent on a shrimp pattern to match the size and color of the ones I had dislodged under the stone.

The overcast had thickened, the sun had disappeared and the desert was gray. The wind whistled along the coulee rim and shook the bulky sage, but scarcely touched the surface of the protected pond.

I shoved off and rowed out toward the center of the lake, looking down to watch the bottom slowly slope away. It was covered thickly with weeds, good shelter for fish, good environment for their food. And then I began to fish, searching the shallows and the depths with my fly, casting in and out, keeping my eyes roving for any sign of a rise.

But there was no sign of life, and I began to fear that the lake was barren. Still, I was determined to give it a thorough trial, and I worked the fly slow and deep, bumping it along the bottom, feeling the occasional sullen resistance of a weed.

Was that a splash I heard behind me? I turned quickly, my eyes searching across the water for the sight of spreading rings. It had sounded like a slashing rise, but there was no visible interruption to the gentle rippled water. Perhaps it was only imagination; perhaps my desire to see a rise had caused me to imagine the sound of one.

Another cast, a wait for the fly to sink, and the beginning of the long, slow retrieve. And then the line was being snatched away from me, the light rod bowed toward the water and I felt the movement of a heavy fish. I felt it shake and twist and reverse itself and seek the bottom. I checked its movement and it started up and broke the surface in a flash of pure gold and flecks of red. A brown!

The trout fought with unexpected vigor, its struggle worthy of a rainbow trout, until I lifted it clear in my net. It was a thing of beauty, tawny gold with leopard's spots and great red freckles on its sides.

I opened its gullet and found snails, which was no help to a fly fisherman at all, but in among them were a few backswimmers—peculiar insects, black and brown and mottled yellow, that swim on their backs and move with incredible speed by rapid movement of their two long, oarlike limbs.

A year before, in British Columbia, I had encountered a hatch of backswimmers of several days' duration. I had been unprepared for them then, but in the interim I had worked out an imitation—a fly with black and yellow body, black wing and full brown pheasant hackle. The imitation still was untried, but I took one from my fly box and tied it on in place of the shrimp. Casting again, I switched my retrieve from the long, slow crawl of the shrimp to quick, erratic jerks, imitative, I hoped, of the rapid bursts of speed with which the natural insect moves.

Almost immediately I was into another fish, a fine, stout brown that struggled nobly. And others followed, until by the time the overcast had merged with approaching darkness, I had released eighteen plump, golden brown trout, and my new fly had won its spurs.

I went back to my little lake many times, and never saw another angler there. During the first year the fishing was as fine as I had found it on my first visit. The lake had been stocked only once, and all of the trout were of a similar size, varying only an inch or two in length and perhaps as much as half a pound in weight. There was no place where the trout could spawn, and if there were any fish of extraordinary size in the lake I never saw them. But a daily catch of a dozen and a half browns, each weighing one and a half to two pounds, is enough so that any angler should not ask for more.

But the next year the fishing declined. The trout had grown longer but had gained little weight, and there seemed to be fewer of them. Obviously, something was wrong, and it soon developed that there was a quickly growing population of sunfish in the lake, devouring most of the available food.

Still, there were some exciting times. On one hot, breathless spring afternoon I fished for hours without a sign of trout, and I had begun to think my little lake was really done. But I stayed on into the darkness, and here and there in the dwindling light the rises came. Full darkness brought a heavy hatch of midges, and in a furious half hour I brought five fish to the net and lost as many more, all on a feather-light, six-foot rod.

Since then the fishing has continued to decline, and I suspect that now only a few brown trout remain. But still I go there, and the little lake never has failed to yield a few of its treasured trout. And now that it has fallen on hard times I release each fish with extra care and hope that it will be there again when I return.

# The Firehole

Far up among the mists of the Continental Divide, a small, clear lake overflows and gives birth to a river. The infant stream flows first to the north, rushing down through lodgepole ranks and wispy growths of prairie smoke and moonrose, waded in by animals, seldom seen by men, with no hint of the things that will happen to it later.

The stream grows as it accepts the water of uncounted springs and tiny tributaries, and then it starts the first of its great serpentine loops and swings to the west as if unaware of all the rocky heights that stand between it and the Pacific Slope.

It flows into lush meadows where moose browse and bison come to feed, and then it enters the first of the big geyser basins: great, roaring, whistling jets of steam, some continuous, some erratic; strange, steaming, stinking bubbles rising up from the pumice and the muck, venting part of the earth's subterranean fire with grumpy sounds like an old coffee pot; and deep, mysterious pools of hot water, rainbow-stained with turquoise, crimson and yellow algae growths, each seeking its own temperature zone. These things give the river its name: the Firehole.

Millions of gallons of boiling water pour into the river here and farther downstream, pumping in algae, salts and nutrients, acids and alkaloids, as well as heat.

Rich with warmth and throbbing life, it flows on to its destiny in a larger river, and eventually its waters are carried north again, then east and finally south to merge with other streams in the mother of rivers, the Mississippi, until at last the water that first spilled from a Yellowstone lake ebbs out through false bottoms and bayous to the Gulf of Mexico.

Of all the young rivers that grow up to become the Mississippi, there is no other like this one born in the mists and smokes of Yellowstone. It is at its best in the spring, when it flows through the water meadows with their tall grass beaten down by animal tracks and spattered with the colors of fringed gentian, goldenweed and white and yellow mule-ears, blue camas, monkshood and yellow monkey flowers. Rainbow, brown and cutthroat trout live in the river, under the cutbanks and the lava lips, feeding on the rich aquatic life and a host of terrestrial creatures swept from the meadows by the wind.

The river's beauty continues through the summer as the greens of the meadow grass turn to soft, burnished gold. Goldenrod and ladies' tresses bloom as summer turns to fall and thunderstorms crackle and roll over the valleys and drench the earth with rain and hail. Even in the dead of winter, the river still is a live thing, its steam rising above the snow as it carries down its cargo of volcanic heat while spray from the geysers freezes into frosty statues on its shores.

The Firehold is an angler's river, a difficult river that often humbles even the most expert of the experts. It is moody and enigmatic, sullen and surprising, unyielding one day and generous the next. Often the trout feed in such numbers that the rings from their rises merge and overlap, but often, too, the river's surface runs glassy and smooth as if nothing lived beneath it. Wise management has preserved its trout so that it remains something of a mecca for American anglers, a river about which it frequently is said that if you can catch fish in the Firehole, you can catch them anywhere. It has been a friendly river to me, almost from the first moment I saw it, and though other nearby streams may offer larger fish or easier fish, the Firehole is my favorite.

I first saw the river on a fine late-spring day. Alan Pratt and I had gone to West Yellowstone to watch a famous caster in action as he taught a class of novice anglers. We had been engaged to help the caster write a book, I to do the editing and Al to do the illustrations, and we wanted to observe his casting technique so that we could write about it and illustrate it as accurately as possible. But in the process, we also found time for fishing—a stop en route at Rock Creek to sample the cutthroats and the browns, an afternoon on the Madison for browns, rainbows and grayling, and some frantic hours during an incredible hatch on Henry's Fork where big rainbows splashed and rolled for fluttering sedges and mayflies.

And then we came to the Firehole, and Al parked his truck on a grassy bluff above the meadow and we looked down upon the classic river. It rippled gently through the grass, a smooth ribbon of water with clouds of steam from the geysers rolling along its upper banks. The long grass bowed before a gentle breeze that also drove great shreds and flakes of cloud across the sky. It was a day bright with light and color.

We donned our waders and jointed up our rods, then hiked down the face of the bluff and into the spongy soil of the meadow, coming out on the river where it entered a gentle bend. For a few moments we stood surveying it, watching the lush riverweeds swaying in the gentle current, looking for a rise. There was none, and it appeared the river was in one of its fickle moods.

Al started downstream and I waded out slowly and cautiously to avoid disturbing any trout that might be in the neighborhood. There were no insects on the surface and a more prudent angler might have concluded that a wet fly or nymph was necessary, but the very character of the smooth flow seemed to demand that anything but a dry fly would be sacrilegious.

And so a dry fly it was, a size 16 pattern with quill body and stiff grizzly hackle. Through my Polaroid glasses I watched the flow of the currents and subcurrents, studied the channels between the heavy weed growth and tried to gauge the float the fly would follow. In the center of the river the current broke smoothly over a lava ledge, its black shape dimly visible through the clear water. Beneath the ledge was a large expanse of dark shadow, and it seemed a perfect spot for a trout to wait under cover for food to be swept down from above.

I cast quartering upstream, and the fly dropped at the edge of the main current, floated down, slipped gracefully over the ledge and continued its jaunty ride down the river untouched. I waited until it was well below the ledge, then lifted it off the water and dried it with a couple of false casts and set it down again, this time near the center of the current. The fly cocked nicely, the hackle points dimpling the river, and rode the current down over the ledge and disappeared in a quick swirl. I lifted the rod, the line went tight and an electric weight throbbed at the other end.

The fish turned quickly from its shelter under the ledge

and started downstream. I gathered line and increased the strain to keep its head out of the moss, and the fish angled off, seeking the strongest flow. Now I was giving it line as it headed farther downstream toward faster water, but a shift of the rod turned its head and sent it swimming toward the bank. The light rod dipped into a tight arc and the white fly line seemed bent by the water's refraction of the light. Slowly the trout tired, and the line came back to the reel, a single cautious turn at a time.

And finally the fish was on its side at my feet, a thick shaft of pale cream and gold with the familiar leopard markings and blood-red spots of a brown trout. It was a male fish of about two pounds, wearing a proud hook on its lower jaw, and the drowned hackles of the little fly protruded from the bony roof of its mouth.

I grasped it gently, admired it, and slipped out the hook, then held the trout until it had the strength to swim slowly back to its refuge under the lava ledge. In just five minutes the Firehole had presented me with a fine brown trout, and if ever there was a case of love at first sight for a river, this, I decided, was it.

I changed flies and floated another pattern over the ledge without result, then moved upstream, fishing the narrow channels between the moss, bumping my fly along the splayed grass growing out of the cutbanks, but there were no other takers. Soon Al joined me and we walked upstream together, keeping back from the fragile edge of the river and watching for rises. Finally I saw one, a cautious dimple near the grass on the far side of the river.

I waded out, my feet sinking into the soft silt of the river bottom. The center of the river hid a slot too deep to cross, and so I decided to make a long cast cross-river to cover the fish I had seen rise. Working out line, I dropped the fly near the opposite bank and mended line upstream to keep drag from setting in before the fly could float over my aiming spot.

The current swept it gently down, the rise came again and I swung the rod sideways to set the hook. A small, bright rainbow broke water and I worked quickly across the current and released it.

After that, we saw no other rises, and finally we returned to Al's truck and drove upstream near the iron bridge. Here we were right among the geysers and the thermal pools, and the stench of sulfur hung heavy in the air.

We waded down the river within inches of boiling springs, but the water still was cool and fresh. We floated flies through choppy riffles and smooth glides and finally, about a quarter of a mile below the bridge, Al hooked a good fish at the foot of an orange-stained slope where a hot spring overflowed. He fought it there in the fast water and released it, a thick-shouldered rainbow of two pounds or better.

Light was fading rapidly and we had been discovered by mosquitoes, and so reluctantly we left the river to prepare dinner in Al's camper. We drove back along the river, through the geyser basin, and watched a full moon rise up through the drifting steam and the dead pines around the geysers, a scene of eerie and mysterious beauty.

It had been only a brief visit, but the charm and strangeness of the Firehole is an unforgettable memory, and I pledged to return. And I did so, one stormy September evening when dark thunderheads gathered at dusk and sent splintering bolts of blue light across the heavens as we drove into the park. Thunder rattled sullenly, a deluge of rain dashed against the windshield and the smell of ozone burned our nostrils.

The storm's violence had subsided, but a hard rain still fell when we reached the inn at Old Faithful. Nate Reed, assistant secretary of the interior, was staying in the park and had asked me to call him so we could fish together on the Firehole. But he was in Mammoth to the north and the storm had knocked out the telephone wires by the time we reached the inn.

I tried to get a message through to him, listening to the electric echo of the passing storm on the wires as the operators tried vainly to make some connection. Finally I gave up and went to a cabin, where I fell asleep with rain drumming steadily on the roof.

The next morning was cold and gray, with intermittent rain and an overcast that reached darkly down to hide the tops of the highest lodgepoles. I drove out to the Firehole and parked atop the same bluff where Alan and I had stopped before, and rigged up in the sporadic rain. The first snow of the season already had come and gone, and had drained the meadow of much of its color. The wildflowers had been put to rest for the winter and there was only the straw color of the long meadow grass, the soft green of the pine groves and the dark strand of the river running through them.

Again I hiked down the face of the bluff, through the spongy soil of the meadow to the gentle bend in the river, and again I came out where the current flowed down over the lava ledge. The river was dotted with circles from the rain, but here and there along the banks were larger swirls from rising fish. This time, I thought, the river is in one of its generous moods, and I felt the old excitement rise as I applied dressing to the fly.

But this time there was no reaction when I floated the fly down over the ledge, and I moved upstream to cover the rises along the bank.

The trout were spooky, and my first step put some of them down. Moving more cautiously, I left the water and crept cautiously upstream, well back from the riverbank, and began to cast from shore. I hooked three fish almost immediately, all of them strong, solid rainbows, and all of them fought free of the tiny hook. The sudden activity put more trout down, and, hunching over so I would not be seen, I made my way farther upstream where other fish were rising.

On the first float a large rainbow took the fly in a perfect head-and-tail rise, but plunged immediately into a bank of moss and twisted free. The other trout stopped rising and I rested the water a long time, but they did not resume.

I left the stretch, knowing now how the river had won its reputation for difficulty, and drove to the iron bridge. Here among the meadow grass there were small hoppers, and I replaced the fly I had been using with a hopper pattern. There was a rise out in the fast water; I covered it and the hopper fly was taken immediately. The fish fought well in the strong current and finally I released a fine, golden brown trout, and sat on the bank to rest under the brooding sky.

Nothing in nature is more beautiful or alive than a river. Each has its own character, no two alike, and each is worth knowing well. I have spent countless hours on mountain brooks and meadow streams, on fierce, brawling steelhead rivers and quiet sluggish sloughs.

But of all the rivers I have seen, or fished, or dreamed about, there is none quite so special as the Firehole, none with greater frustrations or rewards, and none that reaches out so well to capture the imagination or desire of anglers.

# Hosmer

One of the first casualties of America's march toward
industrialization was the Atlantic salmon. His native Eastern
rivers were among the first to be dammed and polluted, the
first to have the life choked out of them. Almost before
anyone knew what was happening, the cream of the once-
great American Atlantic salmon runs had been destroyed and
their host rivers were dead with them.

Today, only a fragment of the salmon runs remain and
biologists struggle to preserve them in the northernmost rivers
of Maine. Still, after the loss of the American salmon fishery,
there remained the great runs to the Canadian rivers, and to

the rivers of Iceland, Norway, England, Ireland and Spain. Anglers who fished for Atlantic salmon on the rivers of these nations quickly crowned the salmon with its rightful title as the prince of fly-rod fish.

And so, indeed, it was—until less than a decade ago the feeding areas of the salmon were discovered in the North Atlantic and a disastrous high-seas commercial fishery began. Fishing fleets from Denmark, a nation which itself contributes nothing to the salmon runs, began to take immature salmon by the ton and the spawning runs returning to their native rivers dropped drastically. Organizations such as the Committee on the Atlantic Salmon Emergency and the Atlantic Salmon Foundation fought bitterly for an end to this destructive fishery, and after years of work an agreement finally was reached under which the Danes will slowly phase out the high-seas fishery.

But even with this agreement, the survival of *Salmo salar* ("the leaper") as a species is far from secure.

While man's callousness and greed were destroying the native Atlantic salmon runs of the eastern United States, his curiosity led him to try to transplant the noble salmon to distant watersheds in distant lands. Early transplants were attempted in British Columbia, New Zealand, Argentina and elsewhere. The Argentine transplant resulted in a thriving population of land-locked fish, but attempts to establish anadromous populations in the rivers of British Columbia and New Zealand met with failure.

Despite these generally discouraging results, other attempts were made over the years to transplant Atlantic salmon. In 1951, the state of Oregon received eyed Atlantic salmon eggs from sea-run fish from Gaspé Bay, Quebec. The eggs were hatched in the hatchery at Wizard Falls, Oregon, and immediately hatchery workers found the offspring were delicate and difficult to handle. Unlike trout, the salmon alevins did not swim up after absorbing their yolk sacs, and bacterial gill disease killed many of them. The survivors were slow to begin feeding, and the original stock had a survival rate of only about 10 percent—extremely poor for fish raised in a hatchery.

Though these early results were frustrating and disappointing, efforts continued to produce a healthy population of fish that could be planted in some suitable water. The work went slowly and the results were far from dramatic; still, the survival rate of eggs and fry gradually was increased to about 20 percent, and enough fish became available for planting.

The search for a place to release the salmon finally centered on a cold, clear, shallow lake high in the Oregon Cascades: Hosmer Lake.

One could search for a lifetime without finding another place with the fierce, wild beauty of Hosmer Lake. Nearly a mile above sea level, nestled in among the volcanic cones of the Oregon Cascades, it is a perfect portrait of nature, a picture of such breathtaking fragile beauty as to discourage one from entering for fear he might somehow injure it by his presence. It is really more of a marsh than a lake, with two large areas of open water connected by a channel winding through weedbeds, lava flows and pine groves. It is crowned on every side by peaks—Bachelor Butte, Broken Top and the Sisters—dark bulks of volcanic rock topped in the springtime by great mantles of blinding snow.

A stream of cold, sweet water runs into the upper end of Hosmer and eventually loses itself in the porous lava of a blind channel at the lower end. The bottom is of cream-colored pumice, crisscrossed with the tracks of clumsy sedge larvae and snails. Ospreys nest in the tallest pines, dropping in spectacular dives to crash through the surface and spear smaller fish with their razor talons, and in the deep-purple twilight of the spring evenings the nighthawks startle in their sudden, swift plunges. Under the light of a clear spring day, the forest is a deep, delicate, satisfying green, almost velvet in texture. The lake and all its surroundings are a mix of clarity and color, so vivid they defy the brightest oils of the artist's brush.

Before the Atlantic salmon came, this place of bright beauty was the home of ignominious carp and roach, and it was known then as Mud Lake. In the fall of 1957, the lake was treated to remove the carp and roach and the next year it was planted with fifteen thousand Atlantic salmon fingerlings, three to six inches long.

To almost everyone's surprise, the salmon thrived in Hosmer Lake. They grew rapidly, feeding on the huge hatches of sedges and mayflies that come on the warm spring and summer afternoons. Management officials, recognizing the great value of the fish in their new environment, made it unlawful for anglers to keep any of the salmon. Only flies with barbless hooks are allowed, and all salmon caught must be returned immediately to the water.

Word of the new fishery spread rapidly among the fly-fishing community, and in the first years after the salmon were introduced fly fishermen caught salmon weighing up to eight or nine pounds—no larger, perhaps, than the grilse of a Canadian salmon stream, but nonetheless unique in their new Western environment. Even today, some fifteen years after the first salmon were placed in Hosmer Lake, the average fish weighs three or four pounds and salmon of six or seven pounds are not unusual.

Spring was changing into summer at the lower elevations when I first saw Hosmer Lake, but high in the Cascades it still was early spring and banks of snow remained drifted up in the shady spots where the sun could not penetrate the dense pine thickets.

I had driven all afternoon through the muggy heat of

central Oregon, and as I started up the final grade out of the sagebrush and juniper country into the semi-alpine environ-ment of the Cascades, a great parade of thunderheads marched along the row of peaks ahead. Soon they took their revenge against the hot stillness of the day, lashing out with lightning bolts and heavy detonations of thunder, spilling a cargo of rain that brought early twilight to the forest. The storm spent itself in an hour and rolled on to dump its remaining rain on some distant watershed, and the setting sun came out to illuminate the land with oblique yellow light.

The dying light struck raindrops clinging to the pines and caused them to glint like spangled tears of dew. The fresh-washed air was clean and pure and thin enough to make a little extra effort necessary to draw a full breath. The streams gossiped on the hillsides as they carried off the rain and the earth seemed to awaken after having slumbered through the day.

The twilight was deep when I drove in to the camp-ground at Hosmer and got out to walk along the edge of the lake. The sedges were flying and far out I could see the salmon rising, throwing up silver spray as they slashed after the fluttering flies. The familiar excitement and anticipation rose up and spilled over inside, and only a practical voice in the back of my mind convinced me that it was too late to begin fishing, so I resolved that I would sleep no later than dawn and begin fishing as early as possible the next day.

And so it was. The sun had scarcely peeked around the base of Bachelor Butte the next morning when I pushed off from shore and began rowing for the entrance to the channel that led to the upper lake. The channel itself was like the estuary of a slow river, gentle and winding, with thick weedbeds growing away on every side. The water was as clear as the air so that every drowned rock and limb stood out clearly. And then, coming at me, gliding like ghosts through the clear water, I saw a school of salmon—shadowy, gray, torpedolike as they moved swiftly and effortlessly, one turning now and then to accept some small item of food, or tilting up to dimple the surface ever so slightly. I watched them pass, then bent into the oars with twice the effort. Coming out of the upper end of the channel into open water once again, I rowed around the edge of a small island, then stood up in the boat to scan the water for feeding fish.

A gentle breeze blew changing riffles across the surface with flat slicks among them, and in one of the slicks I saw a school of salmon over the bright pumice bottom in three feet of water. They were swimming in a tight circle, now and then one digging its nose into the silt in search of a nymph. Approaching cautiously to within sixty feet, I worked out line and then dropped the dry fly gently over the circling fish and waited, trying to control an involuntary tremor in my rod-holding hand.

A salmon rose leisurely and inspected the fly at length without taking, turning away finally to resume his feeding. A second fish went through the same performance, and then I wiggled the rod top slightly to impart some movement to the fly. It moved just a little, and immediately a salmon had it. It was a small fish, but I played it carefully to the boat and held the leader so that I could examine it—my first salmon. It was a handsome fish, its back showing brown through the water, lightly spotted with X-shaped markings, and a red-blue iridescence to its sides. I twisted the fly free and looked for another target.

The day that followed shall always remain bright in my memory. Before noon the sedges began to hatch, great awkward insects that fluttered with abandon far across the surface and disappeared in smashing, violent rises. After noon the mayflies came on, Dark Blue Uprights popping to the surface in unbelievable numbers, resting in rows along the gunwales of my boat and the brim of my hat, flying into my face and dancing in dark swirling cyclones across the surface. I could see the salmon approach from far off and quickly discovered that they moved far more rapidly than trout and that it was necessary to lead them by a long distance with the cast.

Time and again I would watch a salmon approach from a hundred feet away, cast far in front of him and then see every detail clearly as the fish first saw the fly, rushed toward it and took it boldly in a rising wave of water.

I learned, too, that it was necessary to delay the strike until after the salmon had turned down with the fly, and then, when the hook was set, to hold on while the salmon shot away in a long, long run far across the shallow bottom and the reel screamed in futile protest.

The day passed in a blur of motion, of casting, waiting, striking and playing salmon, of repairing smashed leaders and worn-out flies, of long, exhausting battles with great fish whose endurance was far beyond anything I had expected, of pausing occasionally to let my eyes and my soul feast on the beauty all around. When twilight came with a sudden rush, I started the long row back to camp, sunburned and weary but deeply satisfied, and spent the evening groping for superlatives in which to describe the experience.

Since that first golden day I have spent many others on Hosmer Lake and now I have seen it in all its moods—when the forest changes from green to gray under the sullen light of a mountain storm moving in, when the bitter wind from the peaks sweeps long, rolling waves across its surface, and when the mountain sunset paints it in soft, pastel shades at the end of the day. I have found that it is not always nearly so generous as it was on that first day, that sometimes the salmon are moody and cautious; but I have also had other days of wild excitement when great, silver salmon came in lunging rises,

when a sudden hole opened in the water and my fly disappeared into it, when bright fish have scattered the water in
one jump after another, and when I have stood for fully half
an hour with my slim rod bent in a futile effort to bring a big
fish to the net.

It is nearly all dry-fly fishing, and that in itself makes it
an exciting departure from the norm in Western waters. A
Dark Blue Upright or an Iron Blue Dun in size 16 imitates the
mayfly hatch, and a size 8 Salmon Candy is used almost
exclusively when the sedges are up.

The Salmon Candy is the product of Lloyd Frese, who
has spent years developing patterns for use in Hosmer Lake.
He has devised a series of four Salmon Candy patterns, but the
one I have found most useful is a sparsely tied pattern with a
thin body of dark-olive wool, a deerhair wingcase trimmed at
either end and dark-brown gamecock hackle palmered on the
forward half of the body. It is an extremely effective sedge
imitation, especially when tied sparsely, and I have even used
it with good results on the British Columbia sedge hatches far
from the Salmon Candy's point of origin.

It was Lloyd Frese who once said he feared death because
he doubted that heaven could be as good as Hosmer Lake.
And now that I know Hosmer as I do, I share his feeling that
the good Lord will have to go to some special effort to create
an angler's Valhalla surpassing this one.

It is something of a miracle that Hosmer has turned out
the way it has, and that it has managed to last as long as it has.
Efforts to establish Atlantic salmon in other nearby lakes have
proved largely unsuccessful; only in Hosmer does some
unique, indefinable combination of circumstances exist. Yet,
the success of the fishery inevitably has led to a desire to
imitate it elsewhere, and even as this is written an effort is
being made to introduce Atlantic salmon to my own state of
Washington, and discussions are underway in California to
attempt the same thing there.

One hopes that these efforts will meet with some success, and that the proper measures also will be taken to preserve the Atlantic salmon in his native habitat of ocean and stream. Truly he is a fish that deserves the respect of all anglers, of all people, for if his species should disappear the earth will never know another like it.

# Summer

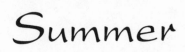

The calendar tells us the very instant when spring comes to an end and summer begins, but the transition is not so easily visible in nature. Spring often is long and cool and wet, and often it is only a gradual warming and drying of the air, a subtle disappearance of blossoms and blooms, that signals the beginning of summer. But once the transition is made, summer leaves little doubt of its presence; for days on end, the sun floats in a clear sky and sucks the moisture from the fields; the grass dries and the gentle winds carry away the thistle seeds in tumbling windrows. Life has reached the peak of the year and begun its gradual decline, and the fragile stems that pushed their way up through the spring soil live out their lush days and begin to wither in the sun.

It is a lazy time for the angler. The trout in the lowland lakes go deep and the rivers run low and clear. The cool freshness of the morning passes quickly to the heavy heat of the day. The night breezes sputter and die, and pollen hangs thickly in the air. The sun quickly saps the strength so that the angler seeks the sparse midday shade to rest and cool himself as best he can, looking forward to the coolness of the evening and hoping the trout will rise again.

The mountains, snowcapped in all the other seasons, are bare now, a distant haze of purple, green and brown. The rivers have long since carried away the runoff from the winter snows, and now they reveal their skeletons—bare, white, water-blasted rocks that are hidden at other times of year.

The trout in the rivers are quick and wary, drawn to the cover of rocky ledges and the coolness of the feeder streams and springs. They rise shyly to the summer moths and the first small hoppers from the fields.

Yet even as the rivers warm and drop and clear, the summer steelhead somehow seek out their diminished flow and enter them. These are clean, bright fish, fresh from the sea and strong, and something in their instinct draws them home in summer to lie in wait in the shadowed canyons and deeper pools of their native rivers for the higher water of fall and winter to take them to their spawning. They are among the most noble fly-rod fish and it is their presence more than any other thing that keeps the angler busy through the summer.

The early morning when the birds have just begun their song and the sky shows the first faint streaks of day is the time to fish for summer steelhead. The air still seems cool and fresh and sweet, the streams murmur softly through the alder glades and the light is soft and gentle. The fish are most active then, shifting up and down and back and forth in their waiting pools before settling down to wait out the harsh light of the day.

It is pleasant to wade under such circumstances, pleasant to be close to the water, to feel its strength and coolness through the waders, to catch a fragment of scent from wild mint growing along the river and watch the dippers at work along the shores.

A long cast drops the bright fly gently on the river and the current swallows it and draws it down to explore the hidden channels around the boulders and the ledges where the steelhead lie, sometimes momentarily visible through the shifting shadows of the stream. And there is always the familiar tenseness, the feeling of suppressed excitement as the angler awaits the heavy strike of a summer steelhead, which has been called the most vicious strike of all.

If one is not a steelhead angler, or even if he is, he may also turn to the mountains during the summer. Though the days are warm and lazy in the lowlands, the mountains are in bloom with the first full blush of life, and the mountain lakes sparkle like tiny hidden jewels, hiding the secrets in their depths. Those secrets include cutthroat, brook and rainbow trout of rare color and hue; bright golden trout and fragile grayling. Their growing season is short, and as they rise eagerly to the small insects that hatch from the cold mountain water they provide a cornucopia of angling opportunities beneath the thrusting peaks and alpine meadows of the Cascades and the Rockies.

Some anglers regard the summer as a season of diminished opportunities, but it is not so; the opportunities are at least equal to those of any other season, but they are of a different nature.

In summer, as in other seasons, the fish are where you find them, and it is those fishermen who have explored the summer rivers and the mountain lakes who have discovered that summer angling has its own pleasures and rewards, and they look forward to summer just as others look forward to their own favorite seasons.

# First Encounter

I was raised as a trout fisherman and taught by my father to fish in lakes and small streams, and for a good many years it never occurred to me that any other fishing could be worthwhile. I lived out my early years within a mile of a small stream where I fished in spring and summer for small trout, never dreaming that in the winter that same river hosted a run of steelhead, some of them nearly as large as I was the first time I had let a line down into the swirling waters of the stream. Indeed, it was many years before I became aware that steelhead existed at all, or understood what they were, or learned that they came into the rivers both in winter and summer, or knew that summer fish would take a fly almost as well as the trout I had grown used to fishing for.

Even once I had learned of the existence of steelhead, I was content to continue fishing for my familiar quarry and at first I did not angle for steelhead in any serious way. Several times in the summer I would try for them, but not with any degree of persistence, and usually after two or three hours of fruitless casting I would leave the river and go someplace where I knew I could depend upon consistent action from the trout. These early attempts resulted in a couple of quick hook-ups, one of which ended in a smashed leader and the other in a lost fish, and in neither case had the fish been on long enough to show what it could do. And so I did not have the feeling that I had really missed anything.

But gradually, my association with older, more experienced anglers convinced me that steelhead fishing held some great rewards, and so one summer finally came when I decided I would continue fishing until I had taken a steelhead on the fly.

It was this determination that led me one evening after work to the North Fork of the Stillaguamish, one of the most noted summer steelhead streams of the Northwest. It had been a hot, sticky, breathless day, but the sun was low in the sky when I arrived at the river and the air was beginning to cool. I parked the car, donned waders and vest, rigged up my rod and set out along the well-worn path through an alder thicket toward the distant sound of the river.

I came out of the woods onto the foot of a well-washed gravel bar and stopped to look around. On the far side of the river, two whitetail does were drinking in the river. Their heads came up, swiveled, and they found me with their eyes. They watched carefully, then turned quickly and bounded swiftly back into the forest, their tails waving like white flags until they vanished from sight.

The river flowed smoothly out of the east and made a

great right-angle turn at the end of the bar, dividing itself around a single large boulder, then merging below it in a run of fast water that battered itself against a high bank and then spilled into a huge, wide pool.

I waded out at the head of the bend and began to fish, letting the current swing the fly down toward the big boulder, straining to see the pockets formed by smaller rocks beneath the surface, then searching them with the fly. Slowly I worked my way down into deeper, faster water, casting short, then long, then longer still, holding the fly in the current, letting it pause, drift, tumble and sweep.

The sun had dipped below the alder fringe but the sky still was bright and small hordes of insects played over the surface of the river, their tiny sounds lost in its heavy chuckle, and small steelhead and salmon fry bobbed now and then to the surface in a frantic dash to capture one.

Now I was below the boulder in the fastest, deepest water, raising my backcast to clear the gravel ramparts piled up by the winter floods, sending the fly on long casts to the high bank on the far side where the current swept it in a long search along the ledge I imagined the water had carved into the bank. Still nothing came to the fly and I moved down, a step or two at a time, until I had fished through half the run. Another cast, and the fly dropped lightly on the water a foot from the opposite bank and the swift current carried it briefly on the surface, and then suddenly a broad silver shape was there behind it for a long instant, and then it was gone and the fly swept on, untouched.

Excited now, I cast again to the spot, and again, without result, then rested the water, tied on a new fly, and searched it further until I was satisfied that the fish would not come again. And then I fished the rest of the run and the head of the big pool where a hard double-haul was needed to send the fly across the broad water, and still there was nothing. Two other anglers passed, each answering with a shrug when I inquired about their luck, and gradually the light subsided, changing from blue-green to deep purple tinged with pink, and the first bright stars twinkled in the darker eastern sky. Still, the river whispered encouragement, and wrote strange messages in moving boils of current that spread out and dissolved themselves across the surface of the pool, only to re-emerge someplace farther on, moving ceaselessly, feeling sightlessly for the channel that would take them eventually to the sea. It was pleasant just to be there, to think and feel, to reach out with the long rod and breathe deeply the warm summer air. I felt as if I were one with the river, belonging to it as much as the fish that moved in its hidden depths or the birds that fed along its changing shores or the tiny nymphs clinging to its gravel.

It was a gentle river, and I was in a gentle mood, and I felt a rare harmony with my surroundings that one does not often feel. I had almost forgotten that my purpose in coming had been to take fish from the river; ironically I felt as if the river had captured me instead, hypnotizing with its rhythmic movements and dull reflected evening light, its deep sounds and its quiet friendliness. It sang a subtle siren's song and I had fallen victim to its wiles.

Then the reverie was gone as quickly as it had come, and my wristwatch told me that in a few more moments full darkness would be at hand and it was time to go. One more cast, I thought, and I'll call it a day.

I worked out line in false casts, then added power with a double haul and sent the line sailing far out across the pool. I had changed to a dark fly as evening came on and I watched as its small, dark shape dropped in the center of a distant boil and vanished in the shadows, then waited as the line grew taut in the pressure of the current and swung around to straighten out below me. Gradually it did so and I waited for the line to pause at the end of the swing, but it kept moving.

The pressure on it suddenly was stronger, and then the line was running off my reel and the reel was sending up a clattering stutter of protest as the line moved faster and faster.

I reared back on the rod to set the hook and the reel's stutter rose to a scream; the backing splice was gone and thin backing line was whistling out at an alarming rate. On and on the fish ran, and I looked around wildly for a way to follow it; the downstream bank was rocky and steep and, while not impassable, it would be slow and difficult to cross. But even as I contemplated my next move, the run stopped far downstream and the taut line telegraphed the movement of a heavy fish shaking its head against the hook.

Gradually the pressure eased and I regained several turns of backing on the reel, and then the fish began to move across the pool, dangerously close to its downstream lip where it spilled out into fast, shallow water. I increased the pressure so that the fish was forced to swim diagonally and gained several more turns of backing on the spool. I heard a sound off to my left and looked up to see another angler settling himself on the rocky bank to watch the struggle in progress.

The river continued its blissful conversation in the fast-fading light, but I was oblivious to it now; every effort, every spark of concentration now was on the struggle with the fish. It was a big one, of that I had no doubt. It was coming toward me now, reluctantly, shaking its head now and then, turning away in sudden, short runs, but slowly losing ground as I gathered line on the reel.

And then I felt the backing splice slide through the tip guide and reeled in slowly, slowly, until it was back on the spool and there were several turns of line on top of it.

Then the fish was off again, this time on an upstream run that started the reel whining again, and again the backing was running out and the fish broached at the foot of the fast run that glanced off the high bank and flowed down into the pool.

I looked back at the watching angler and was surprised to see he had been joined by two others who had come to watch me try to land the fish.

The run was over, but the fish still was upstream and now I had the current to my advantage. Still, the fish fought for every inch of line, straining against both me and the current, but yielding gradually until again all the backing was on the reel.

And then it was off on the most savage run of all, downstream and across, the reel whining shrilly until the run ended in a magnificent leap, the fish erupting five feet out of the water, a great, flashing silver thing, returning to the water in a fountain of spray and a crash that echoed from the rocky banks above the sounds of the river. It was a nickel-bright steelhead, ten pounds easily, maybe twelve, and I had never seen a thing I wanted so badly.

The fish was below me again, down in the deepest water of the pool, twisting and turning and shaking and sending alarming vibrations down the rod and into my wrist. It was pitch-dark now, the stars shining brightly and an owl hooting softly somewhere off in the woods. A single orange spark from a cigarette marked the spot where the other anglers still strained to watch through the gloom, and I fought the fish by feel rather than sight.

The fish was tiring, but so was I, and I transferred the rod from one hand to the other and back again to ease the strain. The backing was on the reel again and the line was coming in, a little faster now, and I began to back up toward the bank to be ready to land the fish. Now there was only twenty feet of line out, now fifteen, and now ten, and I inched my way toward the shore. And then the fish ran with fresh strength, pulling the rod tip down to the water and peeling off twenty-five yards of line as it headed out again to the center of the pool. And then we settled down to slug it out again, and I recovered line turn by turn while the fish fought stubbornly against each movement of the reel handle.

The strength of the fish was nearly gone and it was mostly his weight and the current that I was fighting now. Slowly he came in, but this time I waited before starting for the bank. The last ten feet of line came up through the rod tip and now the leader butt was showing, but it was too dark to see the fish.

And now I started back for the shore, sliding my feet carefully across the silty bottom, keeping the strain on the fish, forcing it to follow me, easing it into shallow water, now three feet deep, now two, beginning to maneuver so that I could get the steelhead between me and the beach and kick it up on the gravel. One more step, and then—with an audible "pop"—the fly came away. The leader dangled limply from the rod tip, and the fish was gone, vanished under the current boils that glinted silver in the starlight.

"Lost him," I said softly, but my audience had heard. The orange spark glowed more brightly for an instant, then disappeared, and I heard small sounds through the darkness as the watching anglers got up from their vantage point.

"Well . . . next time," a sympathetic voice said in the gloom, and then I heard footsteps as they started back along the path away from the river.

Yes, I thought. Next time. And I snipped off the sodden fly, hooked it into the lamb's-wool patch on my vest to dry, and started back for the car, with the river still chuckling softly behind me.

# Once There Was a River

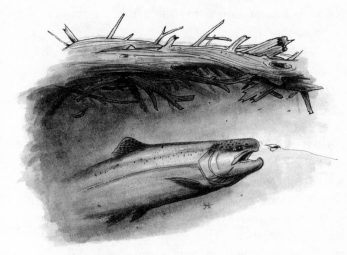

Once there was a river.

It gathered the waters from a quarter of the continent—the seepage from Canadian glaciers, the runoff from the Rocky Mountain snows, the cold springwater of the Cascades—and carried them all to the sea. It was called the Columbia, a name which somehow conveyed the majesty of its size and the strength of its purpose.

A thousand tributaries poured their waters into it, and their proud names are like the roll call of Northwest history—the Snake, Kootenai, Clearwater, Salmon and Deschutes; the Willamette, Wenatchee, Yakima and Spokane; the Blackfoot,

Pend Oreille, Klickitat and Wind. The river and its tributaries traversed every kind of country, from the snowswept walls of the Rockies to the pine-clustered plateaus of Montana, from the gloomy stands of Oregon fir to the desert sage of central Washington.

Even as it drained the moisture of its great watershed, the river also drew into itself the greatest runs of salmon and trout the world has ever known—giant chinook and silver coho salmon, blueback sockeye and sturdy chum, bright steelhead and golden cutthroat, drawn irresistibly from the ocean to the river's broad mouth.

In hundreds of thousands, the salmon and steelhead journeyed up against the river's heavy flow, each race turning aside to its native tributary river, some of them struggling more than a thousand miles until they sensed the familiarity of a lonely stretch of gravel in a tiny tributary high in the mountain foothills. Born of the river, their strength was that of the river, and it was enough to carry them over incredible obstacles to the very place where they first knew life.

The river basin was the dwelling place of Indians with tribal names like the Nez Percé, Spokane, Yakima, Crow, Blackfoot and Shoshoni. They hunted the deer and elk that grazed in the river bottoms and along the higher slopes, speared or trapped the salmon in their season, and knew the river as a great pulsing source of life that provided them the substance of their livelihoods.

The river also was the nesting place for the Great Basin Canada geese, a haven along the mysterious migratory route that took them from the Alberta wetlands to the rich grass of northern California, and it was a flyway for mallard, teal and scaup, goldeneye and pintail and a dozen other species of waterfowl. Herons nested along its shores, bald eagles rested in the tallest trees along its banks, and marsh hawks hunted over its sluggish sloughs.

For uncounted thousands of years, the river rose and fell

in its seasons, dug its mighty channel through the Cascades to the ocean, carried down the waters of its great basin, and nourished the life of all the creatures that lived in or around it. It changed only by the changes it wrought itself, unknown and unimagined by the white men who were working their way slowly west across the untamed continent.

It remained thus until the morning of May 11, 1792, when a small American brig under command of Captain Robert Gray, a fur trader, stumbled into its estuary. The entry in the ship's log for that date reads as follows:

"At 8 a.m., being a little to windward of the entrance of the harbor, bore away, and run in east-northeast, between the breakers, having from five to seven fathoms of water. When we were over the bar we found this to be a large river of fresh water, up which we steered. Many canoes came alongside."

Gray sailed his ship fifteen miles upriver until it grounded briefly and he turned back. For nine days he stayed in the river, trading with the Indians to obtain three hundred beaver pelts and one hundred and fifty sea-otter skins. On May 19, the day before his departure, Gray named the river in honor of his vessel, the *Columbia*.

Nowhere in the *Columbia*'s log is there any sense of historic occasion, nowhere any indication of the significance of the discovery. But after the morning of May 11, 1792, the destiny of the river and all who lived within its reach was forever altered, and the river's days of life and freedom were numbered from that moment.

The Columbia's next visitors from the outside world were the explorers Lewis and Clark, who came upon it overland from the east. Awed by the immensity of the river, the explorers studied their diaries with references to its strength and grandeur, honest in appraisal if not always accurate in spelling. "The water of the South fork Snake is a greenish blue, the north Clearwater as clear as cristial," they wrote. The Columbia Gorge they called a "Great Shute," "foaming

& boiling in a most horriable manner" with "swells &
whorlpools." It was alive with salmon and with "Swan, Geese,
white & gray brants, ducks of various kinds, Guls and
Pleaver." And as they proceeded downstream, the explorers
found the estuary teeming with sea otters and other life. One
day they discovered the water had begun to taste of salt, and
then came that historic morning when Clark wrote in his
diary:

"Ocian in view! O! the joy."

The explorations of Lewis and Clark sealed the fate of
the Columbia. Slowly at first, then more rapidly, the settlers
came, both overland and by sea, and the history of the river
entered the same depressing pattern that had befallen so many
other rivers farther east. White men wrested the land from the
Indians by force or by deceit; slaughtered the game dwelling in
the river bottoms; drove the sea otters to extinction; toppled
the forests along the ridges and the tributary rivers. The
Indians were killed in battle or by disease, the survivors
herded onto reservations. The greatest of them was Chief
Joseph of the Nez Percés, whose people had lived so long in
concert with the river and the land around it. It was Chief
Joseph who articulated the philosophy that only today white
men have begun to understand. He said:

"The earth was created by the assistance of the sun, and
it should be left as it was. . . . The country was made
without lines of demarcation, and it is no man's business to
divide it. . . . I see the whites all over the country gaining
wealth, and see their desire to give us lands which are
worthless. . . . The earth and myself are of one mind. The
measure of the land and the measure of our bodies are the
same. . . . Do not misunderstand me, but understand me
fully with reference to my affection for the land. I never said
the land was mine to do with as I chose. The one who has the
right to dispose of it is the one who has created it. . . ."

Guided by this philosophy, Chief Joseph and his people fought desperately for their beloved land, but they were driven from it by armed troops. Time after time the Indians defeated their pursuers in a long and bloody trek across the mountains toward refuge in Canada. But finally, half starved and frozen, they stopped to rest only a day's march from their goal. And there they were attacked and broken in a one-sided fight in the lonely Montana hills.

The survivors, including Chief Joseph, eventually were confined to a reservation, and the chief died there. On his tombstone it says he died of a broken heart.

In less than a century and a half, the river was tamed and all its native life had been destroyed or broken to the will of man. Recognizing the raw strength of the river, men built dams and drew upon it to irrigate their fields, light their cities and run their factories. One great dam followed another until now there are more than a hundred on the river and its tributaries. And the white men added a final insult to history when they named one of the dams Chief Joseph.

Slowly the Columbia ceased being a river and became a series of huge, slackwater lakes. Now, from the breaks below Bonneville Dam to the Canadian icefields, there is only one fifty-seven-mile stretch that still flows freely.

Great cities sprang up along the Columbia shores and dumped their wastes into the river and its tributaries. Fumes from the great mills fouled the air in the canyons and the valleys. The river bottom was dredged to make way for barges and ships, and its banks were buried in spoil from the dredges. Mighty steel bridges spanned the river to carry a growing cargo of rail and vehicular traffic. The rising reservoir waters drowned the nesting areas of the waterfowl and destroyed the winter range of the surviving game.

The dams blocked many of the steelhead and salmon runs from their native tributaries, and many of the surviving fish met death in commercial fishing nets. Alien species were introduced to prey upon and compete with the native runs of fish. Poison and pollution took a toll.

The virgin timber was stripped from the hillsides, so when the winter snows melted and the spring rains came, the tributaries flooded and carried the topsoil away in rushing torrents that filled the mainstem. The great surge of water spilled its way over dam upon dam in such volume that it became supersaturated with air, drawing it down into the depths of the reservoir pools. And there a strange new threat developed: The supersaturated water flowed through the gills of steelhead and salmon so that their own blood became supersaturated, and when they swam to shallow water, bubbles of air formed in their bloodstreams and they died by the thousands of bursting hearts or ruptured eyeballs.

Even the fish reared in hatcheries to replace those runs exterminated by the dams were slaughtered by the strange new environmental disease.

And still the destruction goes on. The "Great Shute" and the "swells & whorlpools" now lie deep beneath a placid reservoir. Transmission lines stretch away in barren streaks from the dams. Ancient Nez Percé pictographs, painted on the river rocks to guide Indian fishermen to a safe crossing, were shattered by a dynamite blast to clear the way for a county road. The ancient rockshelter at Marmes, site of the earliest human dwelling place yet discovered in the Western Hemisphere, disappeared under the floodwaters of a new dam, its secrets gone forever.

More than fifty other dams have been authorized, recommended or suggested for the Columbia and its tributaries. One of these, named Ben Franklin, would inundate the last free-flowing stretch of the mainstem.

On May 28, 1959, the Senate Public Works Committee approved a resolution to "determine whether any modification of the existing project on the Columbia River between

McNary Reservoir and Priest Rapids Dam is advisable at this time." Particular reference was given to "constructing a multipurpose dam and reservoir at the Ben Franklin site for navigation, hydroelectric power and allied purposes." One supposes that Ben Franklin, in his sage wisdom, would not approve of having his name applied to the last tombstone of a great river.

The dam would generate an average of 3.7 billion kilowatt hours annually. Also involved is an ambitious project that would include navigation locks and channel dredging to make the Columbia navigable all the way upstream to Wenatchee. In the laconic language of the Army Corps of Engineers, which would be in charge of the project, "the dam would complete control of the Columbia River from Bonneville Dam to the Canadian border."

The greatest native runs of salmon and steelhead the world has ever known are gone. Most of the game and waterfowl that once lived along the river are gone. The wilderness that existed along the river is gone. And all but fifty-seven miles of the river itself are forever gone. Yet men still are not satisfied, and plans have been laid to take the last fifty-seven miles as well.

What is the worth of those fifty-seven miles of free-flowing river? Government agencies, in calculating the economic worth of a project, attempt to answer such questions in monetary values. This is a most difficult thing to do. Even the angler who catches a native steelhead fresh from the sea is hard put to explain its worth. It is a thing of value to the soul, not to the pocketbook.

Perhaps the fifty-seven miles would be of little value if they had been treated the same as other sections of the river. But a peculiar combination of circumstances has made it possible for this last living stretch to escape the impact of cities and sewage, freeways and factories.

Below Priest Rapids Dam the river flows through dry,

barren hills, dotted with bitterbrush and sage, unfriendly to human life. In the early 1900s, hardy white settlers carved a small number of homesteads along the riverbanks and cultivated a few small fields with water from the river. Their orchards were rich in fruit and they built two small towns, one named Hanford and the other White Bluffs, the latter after the tall, white cliffs that line the river. But during World War II, the homesteaders were moved out and the towns were erased to make way for great, secret installations where a new substance named plutonium was manufactured, giving both hopes and fears to men.

The area was fenced and closed to public entry, and except for the ugly, gray shapes of the reactors looming starkly visible across the rolling desert, the area reverted nearly to its natural state. Inadvertently, the secrecy surrounding the arrival of the nuclear age preserved the land around the last fifty-seven miles of river.

In that fifty-seven-mile stretch, the river still runs with the energy of its days of freedom. It rips over shallow bars of gravel and boils with great force through narrow passages along the spectacular white bluffs, and splits itself around broad sand islands covered with scrub cottonwood and willow.

Here native steelhead and noble king salmon still return to spawn, evading commercial nets and anglers' wares downstream, fighting their way up the fish ladders of the lower dams, overcoming the effects of pollution and supersaturation in order to do so. The miracle of their procreation is all the more significant because of the man-made hardships they must endure.

Mule deer does still brave the current and swim to the midriver islands to give birth to their fawns, and in the late spring the mothers and fawns may be seen frolicking in the bunchgrass and scrub willow on the islands.

This, too, is still a nesting place for the Great Basin Canada geese, the dwindling remnant of the great flocks that once darkened the skies over the river. Herons still nest here and take flight on ungainly wings at any intrusion. The white bluffs are lined with the sculptured nests of cliff swallows, and doves perch in the dry limbs of the abandoned orchards. Coyotes prowl the riverbanks and swim to the islands in search of prey.

In ancient days, the Indians came to the river here and camped on its islands to fish for the returning salmon. Their campsites and house-pits still are there, together with the relics of their time, covered and uncovered by blowing sand and the shifting river.

Today the withered orchards and the shade trees of the homesteaders still line the riverbanks. The open cellars where once their houses stood are like empty sockets in a weathered skull. And except for this, the river here is much as it was when Gray sailed into the Columbia's mouth or Lewis and Clark crossed the continental divide to find its headwaters. It is alive and free and rich in life, a short stretch of living river in a stream that in every other place has died.

In some senses it is different, and in many ways it is similar to other parts of the river that have disappeared forever beneath quiet reservoir depths. There is, however, one most important difference: This is the last free-flowing stretch, the very last, and once it is gone the mighty Columbia, mother of life, will be only a memory.

# The Quality Concept

"Quality" is a favorite word of advertising agencies. In the context in which they use it, it means, roughly, getting the most for your money.

Yet there is widespread disagreement on what is "the most." To the buyer of an automobile, "the most" may mean the height of luxury; to another buyer, it may mean a vehicle that is ruggedly built and utilitarian. The different perceptions of "quality" extend to many areas. Engineers speak of "enhancing the recreational quality" of a river by building a dam on it; conservationists attack the proposal on the grounds that it will destroy the "quality" of the existing stream. Each side believes firmly and sincerely that it is right, and unfortunately the issue is all too often resolved in favor of the side with the greater political muscle and not on the merits of the issue itself.

The meaning of "quality" is nearly as elusive when applied to angling. Some fishermen measure quality in terms of the number of fish they are able to kill in a single day, regardless of the size of the fish or the circumstances under which they were taken. Other anglers regard quality as the chance to catch large fish, even just one or two a day, and numbers mean little to them. Still other anglers believe that quality means the opportunity to fish in the way they choose without interruption, or the chance to fish in wilderness solitude. And still another definition of quality may include something from all of these attitudes.

But these arguments are largely esthetic in nature and often receive only passing consideration from the agencies charged with fisheries management. These agencies measure quality by still another yardstick—in statistical terms such as "man-days," "catch per unit of effort" and the economic costs of raising and planting fish.

So there is an inherent conflict between the fisherman, who measures his success in terms of personal satisfaction, and the fisheries management agencies, who measure success in columns of statistics. It is unlikely that this conflict ever will be fully resolved, but it seems incumbent upon both sides to try a little harder to understand the other. The greater burden, however, must be on management officials to explore the attitudes of the public, which, after all, is footing the bill.

In many states, the opening day of the fishing season sees huge crowds of anglers setting forth to slaughter trout literally by the millions. This goes on for a weekend or two until nearly all the trout have been removed, and that is the last time many anglers will fish until the next season. The management officials can sit back and relax for another year, satisfied that they have "given the public what it wants."

But is that really what the public wants? Could it be that the only reason the public swarms out on opening day is because it knows that two weeks later it will be too late to catch any fish? Could it be that the public really would be more satisfied to catch fewer fish on opening day in exchange for the opportunity to continue catching fish throughout the season? No one really knows, because the management agencies never have taken the trouble to find out. They have, instead, created a situation where most of the fishing public *has* to fish on opening day and the weekend thereafter in order to be assured of a reasonable chance of catching fish. If the agencies responsible for fisheries management would take the trouble to poll their constituencies, they might find the public is perfectly satisfied with the existing state of affairs—or they might discover that what the public really wants is far different from what it has received.

Of course, there are always a few fish that escape the opening-day crowds, and most states now have a few waters with special restrictions designed to ensure long-term survival and growth of the fish they contain. So, when the opening day crowds have subsided, the really dedicated anglers who fish the season long come into their own, picking up the leftovers or taking advantage of the restricted waters. Frequently, these are the fly fishermen, who have their own very definite ideas of what quality is.

While even within their own ranks there are differences of opinion, it is likely that the great majority of fly fishermen would agree that quality is the chance to fish in their own way for a few large trout, preferably wild trout, in an unspoiled environment.

There is no question that fly fishermen are in a minority, and so the waters set aside for them are relatively few. There is a definite question, however, as to whether their philosophy is a minority one, and it seems quite likely that a substantial portion of the fishing public would agree with the fly fisherman's definition of quality. Again, the problem is that no one has tried to find out.

Realistically, it seems unlikely that any such effort will soon be made. It is an old axiom that, even under our democratic system of government, the government usually is at least ten years behind the wishes of the people. So, what is to be done in the meantime, while we are waiting for the management agencies to wake up to the changing attitudes of the public?

There are a couple of very strong arguments to be made in favor of the fly fisherman's definiton of quality. What makes them especially strong is that they are arguments couched in terms that management agencies understand: numbers and costs.

The first of these arguments is economic in nature. While it is true that fly fishermen are a minority, it also is true that they fish far more often than most anglers whose choice is another method. Fly fishermen spend more on tackle; they spend more on fishing; they travel farther and stay longer to fish when they reach their destination. They spend more on guides, gasoline, licenses, food, liquor and lodging. So, even though in numbers they are a minority, they contribute a disproportionately large share to the sport-fishing economy. Thus, purely from an economic standpoint, their desires should be given special consideration. They should not be given the "leftover" waters that are not fished by the general public; they should be given the very best, most productive waters. There is no excuse for using the richest streams and lakes as receptacles for large plants of hatchery-reared fish that will be caught within a couple of weeks by the opening-day crowd. The "put-and-take" fisheries should be confined to streams and lakes whose productivity is low, because the productivity contributes nothing to the nature of the fishery anyway. The richest waters should, whenever possible, be managed as wild-trout fisheries where recreation may continue under proper regulations throughout the length of the season. To use the most productive waters for "put-and-take" fishing is simply a waste of valuable resources.

The second argument is a statistical one. It is possible to prove that, in terms of total recreational use, the *season-long* use of a fly-fishing-only water is equal to the use of a popular water that is fished out by crowds of anglers on two weekends early in the season. In other words, though a popular spot may be fished by two thousand anglers on each of the first two weekends of the season and be left virtually untouched afterward, a restricted water that draws only a hundred anglers on a weekend still will be used by more than four thousand persons in a season if a hundred anglers fish it every weekend. Combining this argument with the preceding one, it can be shown that the hundred anglers who fish every weekend through the season spend as much or more than the two thousand who fish only the first two weekends and then put away their tackle for the remainder of the year.

The problem, of course, is in gathering the data that will prove the truth of these arguments. And here, again, fly fishermen and like-minded anglers have an advantage, if they will only make use of it. Fly fishermen often are well organized in clubs and in regional or national organizations, such as the Federation of Fly Fishermen. By taking advantage of this organizational strength, they may take the creek censuses and economic surveys necessary to prove their point. The legions of other fishermen are not so organized and lack the means necessary to gather such information or express a united point of view.

The ability to present a united front is especially important. By joining together and deciding what they want, it is possible for angling organizations to go to management agencies and speak for many hundreds of fishermen. Such an approach carries far more weight and is far more effective than separate approaches, differing in nature, brought by individual clubs or spokesmen. This "united front" approach has been tried with great success by anglers' clubs in several states. However, it should be obvious that only proposals within the realm of political and scientific feasibility should be made. In other words, it is necessary first to do your homework, gather the necessary facts, and perform the necessary explorations, and then propose something that is reasonable, something that may be done without a great deal of trouble or cost. Sometimes fly fishermen are guilty of the same offense of which they accuse the management agencies: they fail to take into account the opinion of other angling groups. They must communicate and listen to ensure that their own proposals do not run against the grain of prevailing public opinion.

If the foregoing sounds like an elitist philosophy, I suppose, in truth, that it is. But it also appears to be the likeliest way of preserving something resembling good fishing in the future, to the ultimate benefit of all anglers. At the risk of being accused of snobbism, fly fishermen must take the lead in pressing for more quality angling.

Once an approach to a management agency has been made successfully and the desired goal—some sort of quality fishery—is established, the job still is not over with. Those who sought establishment of the fishery then are obligated to make maximum use of it, or they are likely to lose it later, or lose the opportunity to make further gains.

This is one of the hardest things for fly fishermen to accept. Once they have fought the political battle necessary to gain the fishing they desire, it is natural for them to be protective of it and to resent its use by increasing numbers of anglers. This, however, is an extremely shortsighted attitude. Rather than going out of their way to be secretive about such a fishery, anglers should do their best—within reason—to publicize it and ensure its use. Not only is this the surest way of keeping it for the future, but it also is the single most powerful argument in favor of the establishment of additional quality fisheries. Management officials, once they see the success and increasing use of an initial quality fishery, will be that much easier to sell on the need for more of them.

A case in point is that of Lenice Lake, in the Columbia Basin, about which I will write more later. At the request of fly-fishing clubs in Washington State, Lenice was established as a quality lake with only artificial lures permitted and a limit of three trout a day over twelve inches.

Lenice was an instant success, and its outstanding fishing led to publicity first in the local papers, then in regional magazines and finally in some of the national sporting magazines. The publicity inevitably led to greatly increased use, so that the lake was crowded every weekend throughout the season. This caused quite a bit of resentment among the anglers who had first worked on the project, but the heavy usage of the lake made it obvious that considerable numbers of people were interested in such fishing, and so the Game Department placed the same restrictions on three other lakes nearby. What had started as an effort to reserve a single lake for quality angling had grown suddenly into a chain of four lakes.

Another argument in favor of quality fisheries that seems to be gaining increasing acceptance is that some sort of special regulations are needed to protect dwindling populations of native, naturally spawning fish. The success of fly-fishing-only regulations on the Firehole and Madison rivers are outstanding examples of this. And Hosmer Lake, of which I have written elsewhere in this book, is an example of how an exotic, high-quality fishery may attract anglers from many states, thus providing a considerable economic asset to the state and community in which it is located.

Unquestionably, it has been difficult for fly fishermen

and those who share their concept of quality to gain the type of fishing they desire. Yet it now is clear that the tide is in their favor, that public concern over the future of angling is growing, that quality fishing indeed works and is economically feasible, and that, in the final analysis, it may be the only way we shall ever preserve any semblance of fishing in the future. Today there also are more fly fishermen and more anglers of kindred spirit than ever before, and whereas fly fishing once was regarded as an exclusive sport for a privileged few, it now is growing in public favor and is gaining widespread acceptance as the angling method most consistent with the conservation and wise use of fishery resources.

So the concept of quality is receiving greater understanding and the work is easier today than it was just a few years ago. Still, there is much to be done, and anglers who are concerned about the future of their sport had better be up and about doing it. The sport now stands on the threshold of achieving the kind of fishing that all men dream about, if only enough anglers are strong enough in their dedication to see it through. The choice for the future seems clear: quality fishing, or none at all.

# The Brook Trout
# in the West

When the first colonists landed on the Eastern shores, they found the shadowed pools of the New England streams occupied by a strange, wild trout. It was colored in blue and ivory, in salmon pink and silver, with little jewels of red and yellow on its sides, and it was a willing taker of the primitive baits and flies of that ancient time.

Perhaps a little homesick for the remembered trout of the Old Country, the colonists named the new fish "brook trout," though in actuality it was a char. It was abundant in all the watersheds from the Carolinas to Quebec and inland to the Great Lakes drainage, and the first fly fishermen in this country cut their teeth on brook trout. It was the brook trout that inspired some of America's first contributions to angling literature. It was the fish of George Washington Bethune, Frank Forester, Robert Barnwell Roosevelt, Thaddeus Norris and other pioneer American angling writers.

The brook trout held its own in the East until the industrial revolution was well underway, and then quickly it was gone. Its habitat was destroyed in the short space of a few years as forests gave way to factories and cities and streams were blocked by dams and stained by pollution.

Before the sudden assault of industrialization, the brook trout melted away like snow before the summer sun, and by 1890 it had been driven into the far headwaters of the Eastern streams, where it holds forth still in the springs and tiny feeder creeks that are the beginnings of rivers. The brown trout, more hardy and adaptable, has taken over most of the brook trout's former range that has not been left totally unfit for fish to live in.

But even as the brook trout was dying in its native Eastern rivers, transplants were being made to new waters in the West—the high mountain tarns of the Rockies and the beaver ponds and marshes of the coastal plain. And today the brookie is plentiful in the streams, lakes and ponds of the Western states and Canadian provinces.

In the high mountain lakes of the West, the brook trout grows typically bright and firm with neon spots of red and yellow. It does not often reach large size in the high lakes with their short growing seasons and sparse insect life, but no other waters grow fish with flesh so firm and sweet.

In contrast, beaver-dam trout are apt to be dark from the cedar-stained waters in which they live, and the live, bright colors of the mountain trout are seldom found in the acid waters of the coastal forests. But such trout also are often apt to be large, growing deep and fat on abundant midge pupae and the populous nymphs of dragon and damsel flies.

Even so, the brook trout is not universally popular in its new Western home. He is generally conceded to be an easier fish to take than the native rainbows and cutthroats or the imported brown, and though he fights stubbornly his struggle pales in comparison with the spectacular rainbow. The brook trout breeds under a wider variety of circumstances than the native fish and consequently frequently overpopulates its range, and—perhaps because it is not native to the country—its growth rate never seems quite equal to the native species. Confronted with a choice of fishing for rainbow, cutthroat or brook trout, the typical Western angler is likely to put the brookie at the bottom of his list. The consequence of that is that good brook-trout waters seldom receive the same pressure as their counterparts occupied by other species.

These are all valid criticisms of the brook trout in the West. I have found it to be easier to catch than other species, not quite so sporting on the line, frequently too numerous, and usually slower to reach good size. But I also have found it to be a fish of unique beauty, and even if it does not fight quite so well as other species, it still is a worthy adversary on light tackle.

It was a search for this adversary that took me one late summer day down a heather-covered slope to the shore of Bagley Lake. The dark, square bulk of Table Mountain loomed up overhead, and behind us, up on the ridge, skiers left thin, twisted tracks in the snow.

The trail down to the lake still was covered in spots by aging drifts of snow, and the warm summer sun had brought the mosquitoes forth to hover around the dwarfed alpine firs and spruce that reared above the thick clumps of heather and the ripening blueberries. A bridge of frozen snow still covered the inlet to the lake, and a marmot whistled, high and clear, on the far shore.

The lake was clear as only mountain lakes can be, and the sun outlined every bit of broken shale on its bottom. It seemed impossible that trout could live in such water and not be visible at every glance, but there was no sign of life.

I made my way carefully over the snow bridge across the inlet while Joan, my wife, hiked farther up to the point where the inlet stream vanished under the snow, and began fishing there. I found a spot where the shoreline was free of snow and little buttercups grew in the meadow grass, and I jointed up the small rod and attached a little nymph to a long leader and floating line. My first cast carried into the invisible current from the inlet; the line drifted down with the gentle flow, then came to a sudden and suspicious stop. I lifted the rod tip and felt the throb of a fish and simultaneously I saw it turn, the first sign of a fish I had seen in the clear water. The brook trout tumbled out of the water in a flash of crimson spots and spray, and just as quickly it was gone. I had been too slow to strike and the hook had not been firmly set.

Then I heard a shout from Joan; her rod was bent and plunging, and moments later a fine brookie was thrashing on the wet gravel at her feet. She had let the current carry her fly down into the darkness beneath the snow bridge, and there, hidden in a little cavern in the ice, the trout had taken it. He was the best of all the trout we were to take that day, and we admired his brilliant dress against the backdrop of the snow.

I cast again, and the current carried the fly out into the lake, over a waterlogged limb on the bottom. Every detail was plainly visible through the clear water as a brook trout appeared from under the sunken limb, rose leisurely through ten feet of water and intercepted the drifting nymph in a subtle, sipping rise. To that point the whole act had appeared as if it had been filmed in slow motion, but the trout turned with a quick flash and leaped at the first feel of the hook. And then every motion of its struggle was visible as it vainly sought the sanctuary of the limb from under which it had first appeared.

And that was the way it went for an hour or more, with nearly every cast greeted by a leisurely rise followed by a dogged struggle, with every strike and turn, every twist and jump clearly visible from the first to the last. And when it was over, half a dozen brook trout lay side by side in the snow and we had released many others.

We placed the trout in a wicker creel on a bed of little sword ferns and moist meadow clover and packed handfuls of snow around them before we started back up the steep slope. The top of the ridge was crowded with skiers on their way to the slopes, and we walked to the foot of the run and watched the graceful skiers coming down with shouts of glee cut short as they plunged into a pool of ice water at the bottom. Helping hands and laughing faces greeted them as they emerged from the glacial water, and hands thrust out mugs of beer from kegs buried in the snow. And while hundreds skied and watched and laughed, we had been alone on the lake only a few hundred yards away.

Of all the places I have found brook trout, perhaps the favorite is Leech Lake, a little snowline lake at the summit of White Pass in the Cascades. It is restricted to fly fishing only, and it is ideally suited to the fly. A shallow lake with thick weedbeds growing within a few inches of the surface and sheltering deadfalls around its shore, it provides superb angling from ice-out to freeze-up. The trout never are very large, but always there are many of them, and they are as bright and brilliantly colored as any fish I have ever seen.

On our first visit we arrived late at night and drove the Jeep through the trees until we could see pale moonlight flashing on the water. We made camp on the shore and slept in the open under fragrant boughs of fir, and in the morning I came awake and stared into the startled eyes of a camp robber that was walking up my sleeping bag. The handsome bird took quick flight, and I looked beyond it to the layer of steam that was rising from the calm surface of the lake. Behind the lazy layers of floating steam came the splashing sounds of feeding trout.

Breakfast was a hurried affair, but still the rise had stopped before I was on the water. I spent the morning exploring the lake, casting off the weedbed around the outlet stream, probing the hole at the foot of the rockslide at its western end, dropping the fly around the deadfalls along the shore. Before the day was out I had released more than thirty trout, the males beautiful with the sunset colors of their early spawning dress, the females bright with spattered spots of color.

Leech Lake has given me some of the best fishing of all. On one afternoon nature forgot it was summer and a cold wind whipped a sullen drizzle of rain and wet snow across the surface, and dirty strands of dark cloud hid the ridges and drifted through the woods. But despite the cold, unfriendly weather, it was quickly apparent that this was a special day, that the trout were willing as never before, and nearly every cast over the weedbeds was met by a turning silver shape.

The trout struck hard and fought well until it seemed as if the little bamboo midge rod would be frozen into a permanent curve. The brookies were everywhere—in the weeds, along the deadfalls, in the springhole along the northern shore— and they dashed in twos and threes to strike at my imitation of a damselfly nymph. Once I hooked fish on eleven consecutive casts, something which never has happened to me before or since, and when the afternoon grew prematurely dark in the overcast and the rain, I had released more than a hundred trout.

My friend Ward McClure scoffed in disbelief at the total, and so the next weekend we went there together with a small wager as to who could catch the most trout.

At first it looked as if it would be one of those days that

are best forgotten: I had trouble with the line and trouble with the long, thin leader, and my casts never seemed to fall quite on target. Even when things went well it seemed as if the trout were determined to ignore my fly. Ward had released more than twenty fish before I had my third, and there seemed little chance that I could hope to win the wager.

But then the tide began to change. I found brook trout feeding near the springhole, and they began to come almost as willingly as they had the time before.

The same damselfly nymph that had worked so well before again stimulated their interest, and while Ward was taking an occasional fish around the deadfalls I was getting strikes on nearly every cast. When the afternoon was over and we compared notes, I had released seven more trout than Ward. The wager was settled and we joined our wives around a campfire where steaks and potatoes sputtered over the hot coals, and drank bourbon toasts to the noble brook trout. And the next morning there were brook trout for breakfast, rolled in corn meal and fried in butter, fit for a king.

Fishing in the beaver swamps and ponds is far different from fishing in the mountain lakes. Beaver-pond fishing is difficult; usually the water is dark and impenetrable, hiding a thick tangle of invisible deadfalls and snags. Where ponds have risen in the forest, groves of dead timber remain standing in them to snare the unwary backcast, and it is not unusual to see the skeletons of trees decorated with flies and strands of broken leader. There are floating islands of peat and thick beds of water lilies, and the trout hide under them and feed along their edges. Herons and occasional ospreys fish these waters every day, and the trout grow quickly wary of any quick movement, of every fragment of shadow cast by a bird in flight.

The trout are difficult to approach and difficult to fool, and because their wariness and wisdom have enabled them to survive they often grow to trophy size and weight. Fishless days occur frequently, but when the angler is lucky enough to hook a trout it is likely to be a large one, and then begins the even more difficult task of trying to land a large fish amid a jungle of dead timber and snags.

A mile beyond the end of the nearest forest road I rendezvoused with such a trout in an amber-colored pond on a dark, rainy afternoon. I had been casting along the edge of a bank of lily pads without result, working the bright fly along the silty bottom, trying to avoid the black outlines of deadfalls rearing up near the surface, hoping for a strike. Suddenly it was there: a quick pull with a sense of heavy weight behind it. Then I could feel the fish shaking its head, slowly and strongly, and immediately I knew it was a big brook trout.

It fought deep and I snubbed it hard to keep it from finding the twisted sticks and deadfalls on the bottom. Now and then a heavy boil appeared on the surface as the trout made a sudden turn beneath it, but the fish never showed itself. Gradually the strong rushes grew weaker and the leader butt was visible above the surface. I worked the fish in close and had my first look at it: short and thick, with a broad, square tail, the ivory edges of its fins showing clearly through the dark water.

And then I led it over the waiting net and gasped as the fly came away just as the mesh closed around its thrashing sides. It was a female, dark to match the water of its home, but fat and strong and in fine condition, and it brought me a gold pin from the Washington Fly Fishing Club for the largest brookie of the year and the third largest in the thirty-year history of the club.

Arguments go on over the value of the brook trout in its new Western home. Detractors claim that it is better to plant the native cutthroat or the rainbow, or more sophisticated species like the brown. But in most cases the brook trout has been introduced to waters that formerly were barren of any species, and in most cases it has adapted well enough. The West has abundant water and it seems there is enough to grant the brook trout its share without short-changing the native species or other imports. I suppose the detractors always will continue their arguments against the brook trout in the West, but as for me, I'm glad it's here.

# North Fork Diary

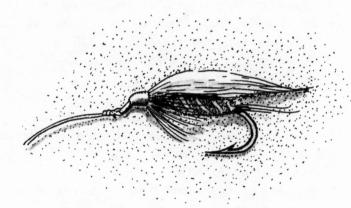

The history of fly fishing in America had its beginnings on such rivers as the Neversink and the Willowemoc, the Beaverkill and the Brodheads. The anglers who fished these rivers developed the theories and wrote the books that still largely influence the angling tactics of the present day.

Perhaps the richest tradition of any river belongs to the Neversink. It was the home river of Theodore Gordon, the patron saint of American fly fishing, father of the dry fly in America. It also was the water of Edward Ringwood Hewitt, and in his private pools he performed the experiments and made the observations that led to so many authoritative books. It was the river of fly tiers who made lasting contributions to the art, including Roy Steenrod, Herman Christian and William Chandler. It is one of the most sacred rivers in the catalog of American waters.

Though its contribution to literature and practice perhaps was not as rich, the tradition of the Brodheads is even older than that of the Neversink. The pioneer angling writer George Washington Bethune fished there as early as the 1840s, and Thaddeus Norris, another great pioneer, came a little later. It was the river of Samuel Phillippe, who is credited with invention of modern, six-strip, split-cane fly-rod construction. George La Branche once owned a stretch of its rippling water, and its list of notables reads like a Who's Who of American fly fishing, stretching over a period of one hundred and thirty years.

The history of the Willowemoc and Beaverkill is hardly less impressive. Norris, La Branche and Hewitt also were at home on these Catskill streams, and they were followed by others such as John Taintor Foote, Ray Holland, John Alden Knight and John Atherton.

There is no stream in the West so rich in history and lore as these four little rivers in the East. Fly fishing in the West is yet relatively new and fresh, and the writers and thinkers who will shape its development are only now beginning to emerge. But if Western angling still seeks its movers and shapers, it already has a growing and impressive list of philosophers and chroniclers, including such writers as Zane Grey, Roderick Haig-Brown and Ben Hur Lampman. And if it lacks historic shrines such as the Neversink and the Brodheads, it soon will have them. And the first of them to be so recognized is likely to be the North Fork of the Stillaguamish River.

The North Fork of the Stillaguamish is not an especially large river, nor is it blessed with an abundance of good fishing water. Yet nearly every major angling writer the Northwest has yet produced has been called to its water at one time or another, and it is the source of a growing body of literature and the scene of development of several innovations and refinements in tackle and tactics.

The North Fork heads in the western foothills of the Cascade Mountains about seventy-five miles northeast of Seattle. Scarcely more than a creek at first, it gathers water from several small branches and flows south through a canyon until it makes a nearly right-angle turn near the little town of Darrington and starts its westward flow. And as it does so, it enters a narrow, verdant valley that is a place of tranquil beauty in all seasons, dominated throughout its length by the eternal, ice-covered bulk of Glacier Peak which rises more than 10,500 feet at its eastern end.

The river runs alternately through white-water, boulder-studded rapids, deep, quiet pools and smooth glides over a bed of rounded gravel. It passes through tiny settlements like Fortson, Hazel and Oso, hardly more than names on the map, and accepts the water of a dozen small tributaries, foremost among them Squire, French and Boulder creeks. And then, at the little community of Oso, it receives its major tributary, Deer Creek, a historic little river that once harbored one of the greatest runs of summer steelhead in the world.

And then it flows on past Hell Creek and Cicero, a river now grown in volume but diminished in spirit as it approaches its confluence with the equal-sized South Fork at the town of Arlington, and together the two rivers flow as one out of their peaceful valley onto the brief coastal plain until they slide into the sheltered waters of Port Susan Bay in Puget Sound.

Before white men came to the valley of the North Fork it was the home of a tribe of Indians who called themselves the Stoluck-wha-nish, a name eventually corrupted by the English tongue into the present name of the river. It was then a country vastly different than it is today. Great forests of western redcedar kept the river in eternal shade, from the salt marshes and sloughs at the river's mouth to the higher hills and valleys where they yielded their domain to fir and spruce. The river hosted noble runs of steelhead in winter and summer, of giant king salmon in the fall, of bright native cutthroat and Dolly Varden char. Great runs of humpback salmon returned to the river in odd-numbered years. The summers were warm and wet, the winters mild, and the Indians—perhaps as many as two thousand of them at their peak—found their livelihood along the river, taking from it only as much as they needed to sustain life.

The Indians were a primitive but resourceful lot, and their way of life was firmly established, ritualized by their forefathers in the misty age of prehistory. They had established a balance with the land, and it was good to them and they in turn were kind to it. But theirs was a way of life destined to fall quickly before the brutal impact of a new and alien culture that had swept across the land, and only the relative isolation of their home protected the Stillaguamish Indians from the fate that earlier came to so many other tribes.

In 1859, other Indians were fighting vainly to resist the white man's march across their land, and the white settlements around Puget Sound feared similar uprisings. In anticipation of possible conflict, military authorities built a road through the virgin forest from Fort Steilacoom, south of Tacoma, to a point beyond the Stillaguamish. It was a crude road, but it offered the first ready access to white men other than the occasional hardy traders and trappers that had ventured into the valley of the North Fork. The valley was included in a county that was recognized by the territorial legislature in 1861, even though a census showed it then had a population of only thirty-six whites, all of them men.

The existence of the military road had no immediate impact on the Indians or their valley. Until 1864 the only white settlement was in the larger valley of the Snohomish River and its tributary, the Skykomish, to the south. But then in 1864 a white man named Henry Marshall cleared a home-stead and built a cabin on the lower Stillaguamish, below the confluence of the forks.

Marshall was but the first, and slowly other settlers began to trickle in. A man named James H. Perkins bought out Marshall, who seemed to be perpetually ill, and Perkins traded with the Indians and began to log the giant cedars that grew virtually in his back yard. He prospered and eventually built a hotel and saloon on the river in a community that came to be known as Florence.

Other loggers moved to the area and established small camps. The price of logs ranged from five to ten dollars a thousand board feet, and the mighty cedars were felled and sold as quickly as the loggers could cut them. Other settlers moved into the logged-off areas and began to farm. Working with shovels, plows and teams of oxen, they drained the salt marches and the sloughs near the river's mouth, built dikes and levees and planted their crops in the rich soil left by the river.

In early June, 1884, a wagon road was completed to the Stillaguamish Valley, and land hunters immediately flocked in. By 1886 the valley was considered one of the most prosperous on Puget Sound, with rich crops and heavy timber harvests that lined the pockets of many of its residents. But it was not a prosperous time for the valley's native inhabitants. They had yielded their land easily, sometimes for small sums, sometimes for nothing. They died from the white man's diseases and got drunk on his cheap whiskey, and the simple, ordered life they always had known suddenly was shattered and confused.

Logging camps sprang up along the North Fork valley, paying better wages than other nearby camps, cutting the timber, hauling it with oxen to the river, floating it down to the sawmills.

By 1889 the valley was thickly settled as far east as

Darrington, and a year later a railroad was punched into the valley from the town of Snohomish to the south. In 1890, the town of Arlington at the confluence of the North and South Forks had a population of fifty people. Fifteen years later it had grown to nearly two thousand.

In 1901, a spur railroad was built along the North Fork to Darrington, and what had been a settlement became a town. Other small communities grew up around sawmills and stores along the railroad and the river. At the point where Deer Creek flowed out of the hills a post office was built and named in honor of John B. Allen, a representative in Congress. Later, to avoid confusion with another town named Allyn, the Post Office arbitrarily changed the name of the little community to Oso, which it remains today.

By the turn of the century, the valley of the North Fork had been changed completely. The timber all had been stripped from the coastal plains, never to grow there again. Farms thrived where once the gloomy forests stood, and cornfields grew where the cutthroat had once foraged on the salt flats. The valley itself had been cleared of timber and planted with crops and orchards, the sawmill towns prospering briefly like gold-mining camps, then fading quickly into rusting, rotting obscurity. The Indians were dead or driven from their lands, less than a hundred surviving and few of those retaining the pure bloodline of their tribe.

The white men had bent the land and its people to their will, and having done that they began to turn their attention to the river. Formerly it had served first as a convenient route of transportation, then as a highway for floating logs to the mills. The railroad eliminated both uses, and as the frontier boundaries fell back, the settlers became more comfortable in their homes and occupations and began to seek their sport in the river.

There is little early record of sport fishing on the river. The Indians fished only for food, and though white fishermen captured the returning salmon in the salt water, the steelhead run had been largely ignored by everyone. Yet the North Fork hosted a great run of summer steelhead, one of the few rivers in the area to have such a run. The bright summer fish ran to the mouth of Deer Creek and held there in the pools and riffles until it was time to run up the creek itself, back into the trackless wilderness where the loggers had yet to reach. Deer Creek flowed in a succession of great, deep pools and around huge boulders, through a shaded canyon where the steelhead could rest through the long months before their spawning. No one knows the original size of that great native run, but there is little doubt that it was one of the finest summer runs in the world, perhaps the finest of them all.

Even so, it escaped all but local attention until 1918, when Zane Grey, the famous Western novelist, arrived in Seattle on his way to Campbell River to fish for tyee (chinook) salmon.

In *Tales of Fresh-Water Fishing,* Grey wrote:

"From several of the fishing tackle dealers, who kindly lent us all the assistance in their power, we got vague information about the wonderful steelhead fishing in Deer Creek. Not one of them, however, had been there. They showed us Deer Creek on the map and claimed that it was almost inaccessible. But if we could get there!

". . . At length we met the best two steelhead anglers in Seattle—Hiller and Van Tassel. They vouched for the marvelous fishing we might find in Deer Creek—if we could get there."

But it developed that neither Hiller nor Van Tassel had been there. However, one of their favorite steelhead pools was in the North Fork of the Stillaguamish at the mouth of Deer Creek. They told Grey the pool recently had been filled with fish, but they had disappeared into the creek after a rain.

Grey and his party went with Hiller and Van Tassel to Arlington, and from there they went to the North Fork.

"Before six o'clock we reached the Stillaguamish, a limpid little river, rushing and placid by turns." And the pool they elected to try was the one at the mouth of Deer Creek.

Hiller and Van Tassel were bait fishermen—the fly being almost unknown in that area at that time—but they used fly rods and "enameled silk lines, the same as those used for fly casting; a short heavy gut leader; . . . a sinker that would roll on the bottom with the current, and very small hooks."

"For bait a small ball of fresh salmon eggs that hid the hook was essential. They strapped a wire or canvas basket, large as a small dishpan, to their waists. . . .

"The use of the basket was unique. I was indeed curious about it. Van Tassel waded knee-deep into the water, put on a bait, and stripping off the reel a goodly length of line, which fell in coils into the basket, he gave his rod a long side sweep and flip and sent that bait clear across the stream. It was an admirable performance, and far from easy, as we anglers soon learned."

This, so far as I know, is the first mention in print of the "stripping basket" that later became popular on the North Fork and many other rivers. It was, at first, an invention peculiar to the North Fork, where it was used only by bait fishermen. But later it was adopted almost exclusively by fly fishermen, who used it to store loose coils of line before making the long casts so often necessary in steelhead fishing, and so difficult to perform when many coils of line are held in the hand. It was the first refinement to emerge from the North Fork, though its popularity has declined since the introduction of the shooting head as a substitute for casting the whole fly line.

Grey and his party caught no fish in the North Fork that day, and they went on to a little logging settlement on Lake McMurray to the north. There they engaged a guide who said he knew the way to Upper Deer Creek. The trip was filled with adventure, beginning on a battered logging train that carried them over rickety, wobbling trestles and once running off the track before they got to the end of the line. After an overnight hike, Grey wrote, "At last we descended to a point where, from under the giant cedars, we could look down upon Deer Creek. A beautiful, green-and-white stream, shining here, dark and gleaming there, wound through a steep-walled canyon. It was worth working for. What struck me at once was the wonderful transparency of the water and the multitude of boulders, some of them huge.

". . . Deer Creek was the most beautiful trout water I had ever seen. Clear as crystal, cold as ice, it spoke eloquently of the pure springs of the mountain fastnesses. . . ."

During his second day on the stream, Grey hooked the first steelhead of his life: "A dark gleam shot into the shallow water. How swift! Then it changed to a silver flash with glints of red. I saw a big fish swoop up and then come clear out into the air—a steelhead, savage and beautiful, fight in every line of his curved body." It was the beginning of a long acquaintance with steelhead that later would take Grey to the Rogue River, which he made famous with his writing.

After Grey's departure, Deer Creek remained inaccessible to all but foot travel, though each year the loggers pushed the forests farther back and closer to the stream. The next angler of stature to visit the area was Roderick Haig-Brown, who came as a member of a logging survey crew in 1927. Fresh from his native England, Haig-Brown knew little of the steelhead then and his first attempt at fishing for them in the Stillaguamish—like Zane Grey's—met with failure. But Haig-Brown, too, was attracted by exciting tales of big steelhead in Deer Creek, and on a June weekend he hiked through the forest to the stream, later describing the experience in his beautiful classic, A River Never Sleeps:

"The river was a lot bigger than the word 'creek' had led

me to expect," he wrote, "and it was beautiful, clear and bright and fast, tumbled on rocks and gravel bars." He caught many strange fish, disappointing both in appearance and in fight, discovering only later that they were Dolly Varden.

Then, late on his second day astream, he hooked a steelhead and lost it after the third wild jump, and knew then that the exciting tales he had heard were true. A few weeks later Haig-Brown landed his first steelhead, a seven-pounder, and he went on to write lovingly and well of these great seagoing trout.

In 1929, another angler came to the river, one who was destined to have a profound influence on it in later years. This was Enos Bradner, then on his first trip to the West Coast from his native Midwest. Liking the country he saw, Bradner decided to return and opened a bookshop in Seattle. During periods when business was slow, he studied maps of the area and spent the weekends exploring the waters he had seen listed on the maps.

In 1934 came the first suggestion that Deer Creek and the North Fork deserved something better than unlimited fishing by unlimited means. The Snohomish County Sportsmen's Association proposed that Deer Creek and one mile of the North Fork be restricted to fly fishing only, an idea that was revolutionary at the time. The proposal was quickly accepted by the State Game Commission, but led just as quickly to a public protest by bait fishermen and property owners in the Stillaguamish Valley. Faced with this opposition, the Sportsmen's Association retreated, the Game Commission rescinded its order and the river was closed to all fishing for a season.

But the idea that the North Fork of the Stillaguamish should be a fly fisherman's river would not die easily. Several members of the Steelhead Trout Club in Seattle, including Bradner, urged the club to seek a fly-fishing-only regulation on the North Fork. When the club refused to act, those in favor of the regulation decided to form a new club of their own.

During a series of meetings in the winter of 1939, the dissident members organized their new club, and in the spring of that year the Washington Fly Fishing Club was formally established in Seattle.

Bradner was elected charter president of the new club. Little known at the time, he later went on to become outdoor editor of the Seattle *Times*, a position he held for twenty-six years.

His book *Northwest Angling* was one of the first to detail steelhead angling methods and provided the most thorough description of the North Fork of the Stillaguamish published until that time. His pet steelhead fly, Brad's Brat, was developed on the North Fork and since has become popular on many Northwest steelhead rivers.

There were eight other charter members of the new club, and a distinguished lot they were. They included Charles King, Dawn Holbrook, Letcher Lambuth, Jack Litsey, Lendall Hunton, Dr. Marvin Brown, Firmin Flohr and Ken McLeod.

Lambuth performed pioneering research on rod bamboo and developed a method of spiral strip construction for bamboo rods. He also did some of the first research on Western trout stream insects, carrying on an extensive correspondence with Preston Jennings, recognized as the leading angling entomologist in the country at that time and author of the still-popular volume *A Book of Trout Flies*. Lambuth's intelligence and organizational ability were to play a major role in the future management of the North Fork.

McLeod was outdoor editor of the Seattle *Post-Intelligencer*, and a political power among the sportsmen of the state. His shrewd instincts and his influence also were destined to play a part in the North Fork story. It was McLeod who suggested the fly pattern that was to become known as the Skykomish Sunrise, perhaps the most famous of all steelhead flies.

(McLeod remembers a gorgeous dawn that prompted him to suggest to his son that he ought to tie a fly of the same colors as the vivid morning sky. His son took him at his word, tied the fly, and the Skykomish Sunrise was born.)

As its first project, the new club set out to seek fly-fishing-only regulations on a number of waters, primarily as a conservation measure to protect migratory runs of fish from overexploitation by rapidly growing numbers of anglers. Word of the effort got around and new members flocked to the fledgling group.

The club introduced a resolution calling for certain lakes and streams to be set aside for fly fishing only. The resolution was approved by the county sports council, an organization of representatives from major outdoor groups, and was transmitted to the State Game Commission in January 1941. The commission approved the new regulation for the North Fork on January 9.

Then the storm broke. When word of the new regulation got around, it was met quickly by a barrage of protest. Residents of the Stillaguamish Valley objected, as they had in 1934, and the Snohomish County Sportsmen's Association (which apparently had undergone a change of heart since it had asked for a fly-fishing-only regulation seven years earlier) led the opposition of other sportsmen. Its publication, the *Snohomish County Sportsman,* editorialized:

"Residents of Snohomish County were considerably surprised when, without warning, the State Game Commission announced that the North Fork of the Stillaguamish River had been closed to all but fly fishing. Residents of the Stillaguamish Valley were not only surprised, but shocked, for many of them were hardy pioneers who ventured into the valley years ago, carrying their possessions on their backs;

hewed out the trails, made their homes, and developed the valley into what it is today. It is no wonder, therefore, that these citizens should become indignant when they find that an elite set of Seattlelites had prevailed upon the commission to set this stream aside for the use of a favored few."

Meetings were held and petitions circulated asking the Game Commission to rescind its action. The Fly Fishing Club, in seeking the regulation, had bypassed the State Sportsmen's Council, a statewide counterpart of the county group and an organization which wielded considerable influence at the time. It quickly became apparent that an attempt would be made through the state organization to condemn the new regulation.

To head off the gathering opposition, the Fly Fishing Club decided to introduce its own resolution to the State Sportsmen's Council, asking it to commend the Game Commission rather than condemn it. With the battle lines thus drawn, the club began an intensive lobbying campaign to win support for its cause.

With Lambuth acting as organizational chief and McLeod giving political advice, club members contacted or joined dozens of other sportsmen's groups, pleading and arguing in favor of the new regulation. When the day of the state meeting finally dawned, the issue still was in doubt and it seemed the resolution had only a 50-50 chance of passage.

The debate was long and bitter, but when the vote finally was taken the resolution passed, with twenty-nine clubs voting in favor and twenty-four against. The regulation would be allowed to take effect, and the North Fork of the Stillaguamish thus became the first steelhead river ever to be restricted to fishing with the fly.

Despite the club's victory, the opposition died hard. A director of the State Sportsmen's Council charged in the press that "unfair and unethical methods" had been used by the club to obtain the favorable vote. The local Grange in the

Stillaguamish Valley took up the opponents' cause. A petition bearing 750 signatures opposed to the regulation was presented to the State Game Commission. Farmers in the valley threatened to post their lands so that fly fishermen could not gain access to the river.

But the Game Commission stuck to its ruling, and as time passed the opposition faded. Fly Fishing Club members surveyed farmers along the river in November 1941 and found twenty who said they opposed the regulation, seven who had no opinion and none at all who were in favor of it. But two years later, many of those who originally had been opposed said they had changed their minds, and the threat to forbid access never materialized. Gradually, the issue ceased to be a controversy.

To this day, the North Fork remains a fly-fishing-only river during the summer steelhead season.

Perhaps it was fitting that Bradner, the first president of the Fly Fishing Club, also was the first to take a steelhead on a fly in the North Fork after the new regulation was imposed. But it was a costly fish. So anxious was Bradner to get to the river that he was stopped for speeding on the way and had to pay a stiff fine, an incident that made humorous copy in the local outdoor columns of the time.

The club itself thrived and since has grown to more than 250 members, numbering among its ranks three national casting champions and several well-known angling writers and photographers.

In 1945, the Fly Fishing Club persuaded the State Game Commission that artificial propagation of summer-run steelhead was a project worth trying. No one ever had attempted it before, but the Game Commission dutifully built a trap in lower Deer Creek and snared seventy-five summer steelhead on their way up the creek to spawn.

The fish were transferred to a hatchery pond, where they

were kept through the long winter months while they ripened slowly. They proved difficult to handle and refused to feed, and in the end only about thirty fish survived.

But in March, 1946, thirty-five thousand fertilized eggs were obtained from those thirty fish. The eggs were hatched and the fry raised in a rearing pond until, in the spring of 1948, they were released to go to sea. Two years later the first of them returned, proving conclusively for the first time that summer steelhead reared in hatcheries would return to the rivers in which they were released.

This pioneer effort in fish propagation has since ensured the survival of the summer-run steelhead sports fishery. Rivers whose native runs were decimated by logging or other damage have been restocked with hatchery fish that now return in greater numbers than the natives ever did. Other streams that never hosted runs of their own have been given them, again with hatchery fish. And though some anglers complain that the hatchery fish are not the equal of the natives—an assertion that has strong evidence in its support—the fact remains that by far the bulk of summer steelhead now come from hatchery origin, and without them very little fishing would remain.

Unfortunately, that is true of the North Fork as well as other rivers. Deer Creek was closed to all fishing to protect the spawning run and ensure that there would always be a supply of native fish in the North Fork, but loggers finally reached the upper sheltered reaches of the stream and stripped the timber down to its banks, without regard for the priceless resource that spawned in its gravel.

Debris was pushed into the once-transparent pools and eroded topsoil washed thickly down from the ravished banks. Herbicides were sprayed along the banks to prevent the growth of alder in the wake of logging, and they also washed into the once pure, sweet water of the stream. Upper Deer

Creek became a desolate, battlefield landscape, and in the short space of a few years one of the greatest summer steelhead runs every known was gone.

Even today, years after the initial onslaught, the logging and spraying continue. A few hardy steelhead still return each year, but they are a pitiful remnant of the original run. In high water, Deer Creek runs in a brown flood with the washed-away topsoil from its upper banks, and in the late-summer months its flow is reduced to a bare trickle, ten degrees warmer than the North Fork itself. Even if the senseless destruction of the watershed is checked, it will take generations before the Deer Creek of Zane Grey and Roderick Haig-Brown returns to its former pristine glory—if ever. In the meantime, the hatchery fish compose the bulk of the run, swimming past the mouth of Deer Creek almost as far east as Darrington, and each pleasant summer day draws hordes of fly fishermen to the North Fork.

Like every river, the North Fork has its list of "regulars," many of them concentrated in the cluster of cabins on the riverbank below Oso. And an impressive lot they are.

Bradner, now in his eightieth summer, still fishes the river from his cabin below Oso. Another regular is Ralph Wahl, whose beautiful photographs—many taken on the North Fork—grace the pages of his book, *Come Wade the River*, set to the text of Haig-Brown's *A River Never Sleeps*.

Walt Johnson is a frequent visitor, and it was on the North Fork that he developed the theory that summer steelhead take a fly out of habits learned in saltwater feeding. Johnson articulated his theory in a concise treatise published in *The Flyfisher* magazine, and has developed a series of fly patterns to simulate the food steelhead find at sea (the Red and Orange Shrimp and Prawn flies). His fly-dressing theory calls for a fly with a small head for "good entry" characteristics, and suggests that the color of a fly should be chosen in relation to the reflective qualities of the stream bottom.

One of the cabins on the Hell Hole is owned by Lew Bell, Everett attorney and third president of the Federation of Fly Fishermen. Other "Stilly" regulars have included Walt (Dub) Price, angling artist, and Wes Drain, whose beautiful Drain's 20 steelhead fly pattern was so named because it took a twenty-pounder.

Rick Miller, noted both for his bold wading and his intricate fly-fishing jewelry, is another regular, as is Dr. George Keough, inventor of the "epoxy weld" for attaching fly line to backing, and of other innovations. Frank Headrick, Don Ives and Al Knudson are other anglers of note whose casts often fall upon the waters of the North Fork.

Little more than fifty years have passed since Zane Grey found his way through the cedar thickets to the productive pools of Deer Creek, but in that relatively short length of time the North Fork of the Stillaguamish has enjoyed a history every bit as rich as that of the famous Eastern streams in their first half-century of angling. And while the tragedy of Deer Creek yet remains unsolved, the valley of the North Fork is still a pleasant, tranquil place, carpeted with small farms and thriving second growths of timber. In the spring it is a rich, soft green, fresh and stimulating in the cool, clear mornings, and in the fall it changes to a rusty orange and gold, fragrant with the scent of maple leaves and woodsmoke. The train still runs over the rusty track from Arlington to Darrington and back, and local residents say it is always late because the engineer likes to stop and fish the Fortson Hole. It is not the wilderness that the Indians knew, but it remains a quiet, peaceful spot, a side valley leading away from the freeways and the cities, ending sharply at the base of an impenetrable bulwark of mountains. The steelhead return faithfully to its pools, even though few of them still are born of the river, and the fly fishermen patrol its banks through the summer mornings, searching for the shadowy gray shapes lying in the deeper pools and runs.

Its history is short, as history goes, but there is promise of a long history yet to come. And if one's imagination is vivid, he may see in the long summer evenings the ghosts of Zane Grey and his companions, wading in the mouth of Deer Creek, casting with their awkward tackle, searching the dark, rippling water for bright steelhead back from the sea.

# Fall

$S$o the year is rushing to a close, and the shorter cycle of the day alerts all the creatures of the wild to do the things that must be done. It is a time of rapid change, the days suddenly colder, the leaves turning red like the sides of the homeward salmon, the first frosts leaving the meadows silver in the morning.

The lazy days of summer are quickly gone, and suddenly there is movement everywhere. Salmon are in the rivers, leaping and struggling with reckless urgency to find their spawning grounds; the cutthroat are close behind them, more subtle in their presence, resting in the shelter of snags and waiting to begin their feast on the loose salmon spawn. Summer steelhead still rest in the canyon pools, growing restless now as the time for spawning grows closer, and fall trout in the lowland lakes are active, fat and strong.

Fall offers such an abundance of opportunities to the angler that the choice of where to fish often is a difficult one. To spend a day searching for salmon or cutthroat might be to miss a spectacular rise of trout; a journey to a favorite lake is undertaken at the risk of missing a river at its best. Yet, if one must have a problem, this is a pleasant one to have, and the agonies of choosing are lessened by the knowledge that the fishing is likely to be good, no matter what the choice.

As the days pass, the last leaves die and fall into the rivers, sucked into the current to turn and flash beneath the surface. There is a cold, hard edge to the wind, and the rain comes in stinging bursts. The pace of death and life quickens perceptibly as nature hurries to complete its work before the dawn of winter and the death of the year.

The anglers feel this, too, glancing anxiously at the calendar, fishing hard from the mist of dawn to the gloom of dusk, fearful they will miss the last opportunities of the year. The corn and beet fields are dotted with the red jackets of hunters, working over bold dogs in search of the noble peasant, and ragged formations of migrating geese are silhouetted high against the clouds. There is a sense of approaching climax in the air, and it is a time of urgency and excitement, of color and movement, a time of fresh mornings and last hopes, a sudden final quickening of energy and life.

And when it finally is over, there will be time to remember; time to remember the triumphs and disappointments of the year, to recollect the first steelhead of winter, the first trout of spring, and all the satisfactions each season has brought. But of all the seasons, fall is my favorite, when the full design of the year finally stands revealed, when the senses seem at their very height from the stimulus of change, and when there is deep fulfillment for all who love the outdoors and seek their pleasure in it.

# Mystery Lake

In geological terms, it was not a very spectacular event. Probably it would have caused only a minor wiggle on a modern seismograph.

Perhaps it was a great rain that caused it, or a sudden thaw after a hard winter, or even a small earthquake. But whatever the cause, it is easy to imagine how it looked: Slowly, ever so slowly, a part of the mountainside detached itself, a dull thunder shook the earth and there were sharp reports like pistol shots as smaller shards of rock split off and fell away. Moving faster now, the mass of rock began to topple into the canyon, gathering speed, throwing out a hail of great boulders and a rain of soil, splintering the timber in its path, sweeping everything before it.

With awesome force it plunged down the steep wall to the canyon floor, crushed and buried the little river running there, and rumbled on, climbing partway up the opposite slope before its speed and strength were spent. The earth slowly ceased trembling and was still, except for the occasional crash of an isolated straggling rock falling from the shattered mountainside, and the air was filled with dust and soil and spray from the murdered river.

Probably it was days before the last loose soil stopped slipping from the ravaged mountain and all the rock and splintered timber had been rolled or swept to a final resting place. And then the earth rested and set out to heal itself.

The river was damned, but still the water kept flowing down from the higher slopes and made a rising lake behind the mass of rock, soil and broken trees that shut off its passage to the sea. As the water rose, it began again to seek an outlet, probing with growing strength for chinks or weak spots in the dam.

At first there were none, but the water level crept gradually to the very top of the dam, spilled over it and dug channels through the loose soil, sweeping out the timber and the smaller rocks, eroding a path around the huge boulders that no small river could ever move, and in time the river's natural flow was restored. But still there remained a small lake behind the broken barrier, with the river flowing into its upper end, the current pressing almost imperceptibly through the lake, then passing out through what remained of the slide.

The winds carried seed to the shattered slope of the mountain, and alders and vine maples sprang up almost overnight. The alders grew in thick jungles, strangling one another until only the hardiest survived, and every autumn the soil was left richer with the fruit of their fallen leaves. A forest generation passed, and even the surviving patriarchs of the alders slowly died, toppling one by one under the weight of the winter snow and the thrust of the summer wind. And even as they died, the seeds of fir and spruce, of cedar and hemlock, were hatching at their very feet, and the new trees grew tall and straight in the lush, wet coastal climate.

And finally, only the lake and the massive boulders on the canyon floor bore evidence of what had happened there.

It was the forest that first brought white men up the lower valley and into the canyon. Like wildfire, the loggers raced across the coastal plain, felling the great stands of virgin timber. Suddenly it was gone, and they found themselves reaching up into the foothills, driving their railroads into the higher watersheds to haul out the bounty of the hills. They came to the lake in the canyon and saw it not as the product of a geological event, but as a pond in which to store the wealth that grew along its surrounding hillsides. The trees were cut and sent hurtling down skid roads to the shore, and a sawmill was built to retrieve the logs from the lake and cut them into useful lengths and widths.

The loggers did the work with their usual ruthless efficiency, and the trees that had grown up to cover the scars on the hillside were quickly cut away. And when the timber was gone the loggers left, as they had left so many other ravaged valleys, to look elsewhere for new stands to cut. Behind them they left a lake filled with drowned timber and a few rotting buildings and twisted strands of rusting cable on its shores.

The hillsides that had echoed with the sounds of axes, saws and steam donkeys grew silent once more. The sounds of the little river were lost quickly in the canyon walls and a lonely wind rattled broken shutters hanging from the empty cabins. Again nature set out patiently to reseed the tortured slope, and grasses, fireweed and seedling alders sprouted in the cemetery of stumps left by the loggers.

But the loggers also had left a crude road reaching into

the canyon and it was not long before other men found it. Prohibition had ended, and two old rum-runners retired to one of the lakeshore cabins, drinking away the nights until they died there. Hunters came for the deer in their season, and a few venturesome fishermen found their way to the lake and caught the small trout they saw rising in the shallows. But of all those who came and went, only a very few discovered the thing that set the lake apart from many others like it.

Those observant few had seen what all the others had not: that in the long, dark shadows of the autumn afternoons, back among the tangled deadfalls near the shore, there came an occasional great swirl—far larger than the rises any small trout would make. To the very small fraternity of anglers who had discovered the secret of the lake, those rises had exciting meaning.

They were not the rises of small trout, but of steelhead; noble fish that had made their way back from the sea, up the swift cataracts of the lower river, over the aging remnants of the natural dam to rest in the still, sheltered waters of the lake. And there they would remain until the winter freshets rekindled their migratory urge and sent them struggling into the upper river to seek their spawning grounds.

The anglers who discovered the secret were fly fishermen, and they guarded the knowledge well. On weekday afternoons, when other visitors to the lake were few, the anglers would go there and cast their flies among the deadfalls where the steelhead lay. And there, in the silence and solitude of the mountain scene, many long and secret struggles were waged between fishermen and the fish that many anglers consider the noblest of them all.

Nearly forty years have passed, and all but a few of the old alders have died. A new stand of fir and spruce has grown up on the hillsides, the trees still young but lush and beautiful and merciful in the way they have restored the slopes. Most of the old anglers who once shared in the secret are gone, their casts falling on some uncharted water across the River Styx. But even after forty years, the lake remains unchanged, quiet and mysterious in its canyon, and the steelhead still return in the fall to rest up for the rigors of spawning.

The surviving old-timers who have fished there since the early days still guard the secret well, but they have chosen a few trusted members of a new generation of anglers to receive the knowledge on condition that they, too, keep it to themselves.

Still, for years there were rumors about the lake, fragmentary reports whispered around campfires about a Shangri-la in the mountains where steelhead were abundant and could be caught like trout. But the name of the lake never was mentioned, and when the rumors were passed back and forth in fishing camps and on river bars, it always was referred to only as the Mystery Lake.

Ralph Wahl is one of those who has fished the lake for thirty years or more, and it was Ralph who invited me to go there with him one September day. Aware that I was about to be let in on a cherished secret, I eagerly accepted the invitation.

After the long ferry ride and the rugged drive up the narrow, winding road leading to the canyon, it was dark when we arrived and we fell asleep to the sound of rain drumming steadily on the roof of Ralph's camper. When we awoke in the morning, the rain had ceased, but a dark, bulky overcast hung in the canyon and sheltered the tops of the surrounding hills. By the calendar it still was summer, but already the vine maples around the lake were bright with color, startling in the dull, gray light of the day.

A light breeze whispered along the canyon walls, shook the moisture from the forest limbs and sent gentle riffles moving on the dark, mysterious surface of the lake. Otherwise all was silent, except for the slow drip of yesterday's rain.

We carried Ralph's boat down to the water and loaded

our gear, then jointed up our rods. Ralph tied on a fly of fluorescent orange yarn, a pattern he always used in the lake because of its high visibility in the dark water. I put on a bright Skykomish Sunrise, thinking that it, too, could easily be seen.

Then, with Ralph at the oars, we set out to explore the lake. Ralph pushed the boat gently through the lightly riffled waters, giving me a tour of the lake, pointing out landmarks and the places that had produced fish for him and others in seasons past.

"Here's where Enos took a fish," he would say, "and Tommy Brayshaw got a good one there."

Water ousels hopped on the logs and a rusty-headed merganser went about its affairs with dignity. A flashy kingfisher winged overhead on its way to the hunt. Except for them, we were alone on the dark water.

Then we began to fish. Ralph maneuvered the boat expertly between a pair of deadfalls and held it there with the oars. "Put your fly next to the inside log," he advised, and I cast where he indicated. The fly sank slowly out of sight in the dark water, a tuft of bright bucktail and a splash of brilliant orange growing smaller and fainter until it passed from sight beneath the log. "Now retrieve," Ralph said.

I drew the fly back with slow, even pulls until something stopped it hard. "I've got one," I said.

Ralph quickly backed the boat away into open water. The fish followed obediently and I kept the pressure from it until we were away from the surrounding snags. Then I tightened on it and saw its sides flash silver as it turned.

It was a small steelhead and not a spectacular one. It struggled deeply, never jumping, and after a short fight I led it over Ralph's waiting net and he lifted it into the boat. It was a bright hen fish of about three pounds. "Just a baby," Ralph said. But it was tangible evidence that the lake still held its secret treasure.

We worked along the shoreline, casting in among the snags, and then moved into the outlet where the current was noticeable along the shore. We saw two steelhead in among the snags as we approached, and they moved cautiously as we drew near. We cast ahead of them, but neither would take.

Ralph guided the boat around the outlet, pointing out the likely spots and the underwater hazards that could snare a sunken fly. And then, suddenly, there was a great boil on the surface less than sixty feet away. I picked up the fly, false-cast once, and dropped it in the center of the spreading rings of water. On the first pull of the retrieve a fish struck with wild fury and the line burned my fingers as he took it away from me. Instantly the fish was away in a furious run, the line melting rapidly from the reel until suddenly it was gone and the yellow backing line was whistling out behind it.

The fish leaped twice, a magnificent bright steelhead, and then it was in among the snags along the shore and the wild throb of life at the end of the line was quickly gone.

The line went slack and I let out a long, shuddering breath. Less than ten seconds had elapsed from the first jolt of the strike to the loss of the fish, and Ralph still sat with the oars suspended above the water as they had been before the strike. There had been nothing either of us could do to check the violent run of the fish.

I started reeling in, and the line went taut again. But this time there was no life at the end of it, only the sullen, unyielding weight of a snag. And, as we found, there was more than a single snag, and we spent the next quarter-hour following the line where the fish had taken it, first around one deadfall and then another, until we came at last to one where the bright fly was stuck firmly in the rotting wood.

We fished then until it was lunchtime, taking turns rowing and casting, but saw no other fish. After lunch we worked our way down the shore toward the far end of the lake, then turned around and worked our way back again. Ralph probed every familiar spot, casting with great skill, dropping his fly within an inch of every likely resting place. But still there was nothing.

The day passed quickly, as fishing days always do, and now and then the clouds parted briefly to admit the sun, then closed up again, and the mottled light slowly faded as the afternoon died. Soon it would be time to go, but we decided to make one last swing through the area of the outlet. I took the oars and steered the boat carefully through the jumbled snags while Ralph searched the water with his fly. But there was no response.

Then Ralph took over the oars for the row back to shore, and I stood up to cast again. I had not much confidence that I would catch anything after the thorough and faultless way Ralph had covered the water without result. But on the third cast a steelhead appeared from behind a log and nailed the fly with jarring force.

Ralph saw the strike and yelled at me to keep the fish's head up. I put on all the strain I dared to keep the steelhead from diving back into the snags while Ralph rowed frantically for open water.

Luck was with us, and we kept the fish in check until the boat was drifting free in deep, unobstructed water. Then I began to play the fish, and it fought stubbornly in a series of strong, head-shaking runs, twisting and turning and struggling to free itself. But it was well hooked, and without the sanctuary of the logs it became helpless as it tired. Finally it turned slowly on its side and I steered it carefully to Ralph's waiting net.

It was a fine buck with a pale-rose shaft of color on its sides and a proud hook on its lower jaw, and it pulled Ralph's pocket scale down to the 6½-pound mark when we weighed it in the net.

I looked at the exhausted fish and thought of all the hazards it had overcome to return to this lost little lake in the mountains. It had been born in the spring floods above the lake and had spent its first summer there, evading the quick stabs of kingfishers and mergansers. It had survived the difficult journey down the white water of the lower river and its transition to the tide. Then it had gone to feed in some far unknown stretch of the Pacific, somehow surviving the deadly ocean predators that consumed hundreds of its brethren.

Finally instinct had summoned it back, calling it unerringly home across half the earth, through countless miles of strange and dangerous water, past the fatal commercial nets to the mouth of its river. And then it had thrown itself against all the weight of the falling water, struggling through the pools and fierce rapids of the lower river until at last it found a way through the debris of the ancient slide to the shelter of the lake.

And then, having met every stern test that nature could devise, it had fallen victim to my fly, and now its life was in my hands. Neither it nor its ancestors ever had known the concrete of a hatchery trough; it was wild and free, as wild as its native country before the coming of man. And it held the seeds of a future generation, strong seeds that surely would take its offspring safely on the same long, dangerous journey.

I slipped the fish gently back over the side of the boat and into the dark water, holding it carefully, moving it back and forth until its gills opened and closed again in a steady rhythm and I could feel its strength return. And then I watched it swim slowly away, its carmine-and-silver sides disappearing in the depths, on its way to join the other survivors of the journey.

And then we went home, deeply satisfied with the day.

Of course I have returned to the lake, and each time the steelhead were there, and I have waged other silent struggles, alone beneath the shadowed silence of the canyon walls. The landmarks that Ralph first showed me are familiar to me now, and I know them as well as the steelhead that seek their shelter. Still, there is always a strange excitement about this secret place, a feeling that perhaps there are other surprises yet undiscovered in its dark, mysterious waters. Other anglers still come and go without sensing there is anything more than casual observation admits, and the secret of the lake still is safe among those few who know it.

And it will remain safe with me, as Ralph knew it would when he gave it, until the day I am convinced that some brother angler will value it as much as I do. Then, and only then, will I take him there and show him what was created on that long-forgotten day when the mountainside fell and Mystery Lake was born.

# The Plastic Flags
## Are Flying

It was one of those rare autumn days that would be more at
home in May or June or in some other month when such
gentle weather might be expected. I steered the Jeep over the
crest of a hill and started down the rolling slope that led to the
river valley on the other side.

Thick, heavy mist still hid the valley floor where the hills
crowd together and the water rushes down through narrow
stone walls. The sun, rising now over the massive bulwark of
Mount Baker, glittered whitely off the floating layer of mist.
The cornfields along the road had been freshly cut and somewhere in the rows of stubble pheasants were feeding. The

apple trees still sagged under a burden of crimson fruit. There was a moist freshness to the air, and a feeling of change, and it was one of those days when the earth fairly sparkles and it seems very good to be alive.

I was on my way to test a tip about a fishing "hotspot," one of those secret places that anglers whisper about to trusted friends who have sworn oaths not to reveal them. The friend who had told me about this place had spoken of brook trout so large that I was faintly incredulous, but the earnestness of his manner had compelled me to see for myself if it was really true.

He had made a special point of advising me that I should ask the owner of the property for permission to fish in his hidden waters. The owner's careful control of the access, he explained, was what preserved the fishing in his private pond.

Following the directions he had given me, I found the place without difficulty and drove into the yard in front of a tall, rambling, old white house.

Several generations of clothing hung from a long clothesline. Five children ran into the house and three different ones came out the other side. What I had mistaken for a boulder in the yard got up and waddled away majestically, a huge sow grown fat on whatever sows eat. A fierce-looking billy goat bleated gravely at me, and I was glad to see he was tethered by a strong chain. The grass in the yard was worn thin by the traffic of children and animals, and that and the weather-beaten paint on the house gave the place a comfortable, lived-in look, like an old fishing jacket.

A very large woman came out of the house and eyed me suspiciously. She frowned, and I sensed it was a permanent condition with her: The fat had grown up around the lines in her face and made it so. Her hair was tight coils of grizzled gray, and she wore a flowered dress and an Aunt Jemima apron. She put her meaty hands upon her broad hips and took a defiant stance like a professional linebacker.

Her manner was intimidating, but I tried to sound lighthearted as I asked, "How's chances of fishing your pond?" I could see the glint of water flashing through the shade trees in back of the house.

"Wal, I dunno," she said, the canyons of her face growing deeper still. "We been havin' lots of trouble down there. Had to get the sheriff last week. Kids drinkin' beer. He run 'em off."

"I just want to fish, not drink," I said, shattering the image of fisherman everywhere.

She looked me up and down, as if deciding whether it would be necessary to call the sheriff again. But then she relented.

"Wal," she said, "I suppose it'd be OK. You kin put your boat in over there," and she gestured toward a stretch of pasture across the way.

I thanked her, returned to the Jeep and drove to the appointed spot, then unloaded the boat from its cartop rack. I lifted it awkwardly over a sagging barbed-wire fence that stood between me and the pond, then dragged it through the long grass to the shore, taking care to avoid the evidence of recent occupancy of the pasture.

The pond was small and narrow, perhaps a quarter of a mile long. Even though the sun was now high and the day was bright, it was mostly in shadow from the trees along both shores.

There were old alders, second-growth firs and cedar and even a few tall poplars on the side of the pond toward the house. A small stream entered the upper end of the pond and flowed out the other. The water was still and clear.

I assembled my rod, threaded the line through the guides and attached a fly to the leader, then pushed out from shore. In the shallows, the bottom was grown over thickly with weeds. I reached over the side of the boat, grabbed one by the stem and pulled it up to examine it. A dozen big freshwater shrimp fell wiggling into my hand. That was a surprise; I had not expected to find shrimp in this place. Perhaps my friend had not been exaggerating; an abundance of shrimp would surely grow large fish.

I let the boat drift farther out into the pond and made my first cast. The little dry fly settled gently on the surface and rode lightly on its hackles. There was a quick rise and I struck instantly.

There was hardly any resistance, and then I saw the flash of a tiny fish on the end of my line. I stripped in quickly, hoping to release the little fish without injury. Another surprise; it was not a trout, but a fingerling salmon.

I remembered then that the creek flowing through the pond entered a large river farther downstream, a river with a good run of coho salmon. Obviously some of them spawned in this tributary, and their offspring used the little pond as a nursery area, feeding and growing until they were of an age to begin their migration toward the sea. And as I looked around, I saw other tiny dimples as the fingerlings rose to feed upon small insects hatching on the surface.

But where were the trout? The water was extraordinarily clear and the bottom features stood out clearly for fifty feet around. But nowhere in among the weeds or drowned deadfalls did I see anything but salmon fry. I began to row slowly toward the other end of the pond, scanning the water as I went, hoping for a glimpse of something bigger.

Then a sudden movement caught my eye, close in. I looked down upon the back of a huge trout lying deep in the weeds. The familiar vermiculations of the Eastern brook trout were on its back and the ivory-edged fins confirmed the identification. I watched, enthralled, as the great fish balanced gently on its fins, now and then moving quickly to swallow some small thing I could not see. It was one of the biggest brook trout I had ever seen.

I eased the boat away as gently and quietly as possible,

then cast my fly over the trout's station. In the clear water, the thin leader appeared as large and heavy as a telephone cable. The trout, which had seen it all before, moved off slowly and, I thought, disdainfully.

But soon I found others, schools of them, including some even larger than the first trout I had seen. They moved together slowly, up and down the upstream end of the pond, weaving in and out among the weeds, holding now and then in the shadows of the deadfalls, seemingly unconcerned about my presence which was inescapably visible to them.

I tried for them in every way I knew. Soon concluding that they were too shy and sophisticated to rise to a dry fly, I tried them with nymph and shrimp imitations and then finally with the bright attractor patterns which brook trout have been known to take. I tried them with floating lines and sinking lines, with fast retrieve and slow, and with the smallest, lightest tippet that I had. Most often they did not respond at all, and when they did respond it was only to move away slowly, unhurriedly.

As the day wore on, insects began to hatch; chironomids first, then scattered mayflies, then even a few big, awkward sedges. And this was in October: Think what hatches must come here in the spring! With such an abundance of feed, there was little wonder that the trout were slow to take an artificial.

Finally I accepted defeat, and began to row back to the pasture without having had so much as a single strike. Too much natural feed, I thought; or perhaps it was the weather, which obviously was too good to catch fish. But no problem. The season is nearly over, but few others know about this place and next year I'll come back on a cloudy day, or when it's raining, and catch the blazes out of them.

And I did go back the next year; and all along the road there were signs advertising "Excalibur Estates," or some such, and when I reached what I had thought was my secret place there was a small A-frame cabin where I had launched my boat the year before. On it was a sign that said "Sales Office" and everywhere about there were bright plastic flags strung from the few remaining trees, flapping noisily in the wind.

The sow and the billy goat and the clothing on the line and the fat woman and the children were gone. Bulldozers had been there and had done their work around the tiny, fragile pond. Most of the trees were gone, and the stumps and slash had been raked up into smoldering piles. Survey stakes marked with plastic ribbons denoted the boundaries of postage-stamp-sized lots all around the pond. The pond itself stood naked to the sun, and the water near the shoreline was turbid with mud from the bulldozers.

Suddenly I felt very sad, and in my mind I cried for the land. The life-chain that had made the pond what it was had been irreparably broken. No longer would the earth hold the rain and release it slowly to the pond, enriched with the nutrients of the soil. No longer would the shadows of the trees keep the waters cool and protected. No longer would the water be clear and bright. The hatches still would come, but not in their former volume because now the silt would kill the eggs and larvae. Even as shy as they had been, the big trout inevitably would finally be caught, and there would be none to replace them. The salmon fry no longer would have a rich food source to prepare them for their hazardous journey. The charm that had been there in October had gone up in the smoke of burning slash in May.

All this, I thought, so that some developer can realize a small dream of short-term profit. And our children never will know what they have missed.

It was, I suppose, a small loss compared with the vastness of the country. But it was not singular; the plastic flags are flying everywhere, on countless streams and lakes, in countless forests and meadows. Each day sees fewer waters left, fewer places where trout can grow, where salmon can rest or wildlife come to feed; fewer places where man can go to restore his spirit.

October came again. The apples grew ripe and heavy on the limbs, the corn was harvested from the fields, the mist was thick again upon the meadows. But in a small way, the earth seemed a poorer place.

# Duwamish
# Episode

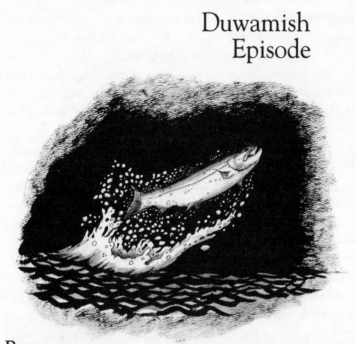

Raindrops chased each other down the windowpane, and a cold wind shook drops from the old cherry tree outside the house. Even though it was October, my favorite month to fish, the day seemed so inhospitable that I felt reluctant to go out into it. Perhaps it would be a better day to light a big fire in the fireplace and set up a fly-tying vise next to it and spend the day there in hopes of better weather later.

That was my frame of mind when the phone rang. Ward McClure was at the other end, calling from his place of work at the Boeing plant on the Duwamish River.

"Are you going fishing today?" he asked.

"I'd just about made up my mind not to," I said. "It looks pretty crummy outside."

"Well, I thought I'd tell you that the river here is full of salmon. They're jumping everywhere. I'm sure you could take one on a fly."

The fireside was forgotten, and so was the tying vise. Here was a chance I had been waiting for: a chance to cast to an active school of coho, to hook one on the fly.

Of all the Pacific salmon, the coho responds to a fly more readily than any other species. But still it is a reluctant taker compared with the Atlantic salmon or the steelhead. Its feeding is done at sea, and it is hard to find there, harder still to take on a cast fly.

Nearly all the fly-caught salmon are taken by trolling flies from boats, a method I do not prefer. By the time they come to the river mouths, the salmon have ceased feeding and are even more difficult to catch. But there, at least, they are easily found, and an angler can cast to them individually and hope that perhaps one in a hundred will respond.

The boat already was on top of the truck, and it was only a short drive from my home to the river. The Duwamish is a crowded, ugly river, flowing through the heart of Seattle's industrial district. It has been abused in countless ways. From its beginning as the Green River in the Cascade foothills it flows down into a reservoir created by a dam and serves as the water supply for the city of Tacoma. The remaining water spills through the dam and runs down a spectacular gorge into the upper reaches of the broad Green River Valley. Here it is crossed by winding county roads, its banks dotted by neat dairy cattle and berry farms. In its middle reaches it flows by the valley cities, Kent and Auburn, where levees and ripraps have been built along its banks. Runoff from a thousand asphalt parking lots pours into it, and in its lower reach, where it is called the Duwamish, it carries down a weight of refuse from the mills and factories that line its shores.

Freighters and barges move upstream from its mouth at Elliott Bay, and freeways and power lines run alongside. A big shipyard stands on an artificial island at its mouth.

Still, despite all this, the river carries large runs of salmon and steelhead, most of them running back to upstream hatcheries. Perhaps they are no longer native fish, but after their years at sea they enter the river strong and bright and they bring anglers to the river in nearly every month of the year.

Finding a place where the river was not walled off by a factory was not easy, but after some searching I found one. Once a house had stood there, before the factories came, but it had long since been vacant and now half of it had burned. Behind it was a sharply sloping bank, covered with mud and scum from the river and the tide which ran up well above the spot.

I eased the truck up to the bank and slid the boat down to the water. Out in the broad river I could see the splash of salmon heading upstream. Huge trucks roared by on the freeway behind me and a passenger jet winged overhead, shaking the earth with artificial thunder. A diesel switcher moved a rattling line of freightcars somewhere near and the place reverberated with the din of the city. It seemed a very strange place to cast a fly for salmon, and I wondered idly how I would get out of the way if a big freighter came steaming down the river.

Directly across from my launching point was the Boeing plant, and Ward came out on the antenna deck and waved as I launched the boat. He could not shout above the great industrial roar all around us, but he pointed toward the far side of the river where most of the salmon seemed to be rolling and jumping.

I started rowing for the spot, and found my boat in the grasp of contending waters. The tide was flooding in fast, lapping at the base of old pilings near the shore, meeting the strong current of the river, breaking into a changing series of short rips and eddies. The river was too strong and deep for me to anchor in the center of the flow, so I backtracked to the shelter of a small point of land. From there it would be a long cast to where the fish were showing, but I had brought a sturdy nine-foot rod, the largest in my arsenal, and with it I was sure I could reach the fish. Some of them were coming in close to the boat, but most were farther out; some of them showed color as they rolled, but most were still silver-bright. Perhaps they would not be as strong as they were in their prime at sea, but I was sure they would give me as much as I could handle. There were fish of all sizes, from little jacks of less than twenty inches to bigger brutes of fifteen pounds or better.

I had no precedent for this type of fishing, no experience to draw from. Which would be in order, a floating line or a sinker? Fast retrieve or slow? A small fly or a large one? I would have to experiment to find out.

I started with a floating line, because that is what is used by the trollers who fish at sea. I waited for a fish to roll and saw one, then cast with a hard double-haul, dropped the fly ahead of it and began to retrieve. There was no response. For half an hour I cast into the ascending school with the floating line, varying the retrieve from fast to slow with erratic stages in between. Nothing.

Perhaps a sinking line was needed. I made the change, and resumed casting, letting the line sink at first, varying the retrieve again. The fish went by me in a steady march, but none of them acknowledged the presence of my fly.

Perhaps it was the fly itself. I had tried half a dozen patterns, and finally I turned again to my fly box, choosing a small fly with a silver body and a polar wing with a touch of peacock sword topping. The fly seemed too small to interest fish of such size, and even if it did, the hook seemed too small to hold them. But nothing else had worked, so I thought I might as well try it.

A large fish rolled and I led it with the cast and began a fast retrieve. Suddenly the fish was there, its mouth opened and then closed around the fly. I struck hard and the fish rose out of the water, a great flash of blue and silver, ten pounds anyway. Then it gave its broad head a single, vicious shake and the eight-pound-test leader quickly parted.

My hands were shaking so that it was difficult to tie on the new tippet and another fly of the same pattern. The rhythm of casting was a calming influence, however, and soon I settled down again. Then, a few casts later, another broad silver gleam appeared behind the fly and took it suddenly. This time the small hook came away as soon as I tried to set it.

The fast retrieve seemed to be the answer, and as the afternoon wore on and the tide flooded toward its height I hooked three other salmon, but in every case the hook pulled out, too small and light to penetrate the heavy gristle of the salmon's jaw. I switched back to larger patterns and worked them with the same retrieve, but the fish seemed to have an interest only in the small fly with the polar wing, and so eventually I tied it on again.

Suddenly, as I was near the end of the retrieve of a long cast, a big salmon came out from under the boat and fell on the fly not ten feet away. Without pausing, he continued his headlong upstream rush with irresistible strength; the heavy reel squealed as line shot out; then the drag jammed, the line stretched and the leader popped and came flying back at me.

I opened the reel and doused it with a fresh coat of oil, then tested it. It seemed to be all right, so I repaired the broken leader and reached for the last of the three polar-wing patterns I had brought. The tide had nearly reached its maximum and sporadic rain still fell. The afternoon was nearly spent, and I knew that once the tide crested the salmon would stop coming.

Fish still were rolling, however, and I chose a large one and made my cast. The fish turned to follow the retrieve and took the fly midway to the boat. I struck hard and felt solid contact. The fish turned and ran far across stream toward the opposite bank, taking great, screaming gulps of line from the reel. This time the reel did not freeze, and the fish still was on at the end of its run. Then it leaped high out of the water, flashing brilliant silver through the rain. I felt its strong, heavy weight at the end of the line, and began to reel it slowly as it worked its way back toward me. Then it turned and ran again, and at the end of the run came a second jump, the big fish turning completely over in the air. And as it did so, the tiny fly came away again, and there was only the drag of the current on my line.

After that, there were no more strikes, and in a few minutes there were no more salmon to be seen rolling in the current. The tide had reached its peak and was ebbing out, leaving a wet ring around the pilings. The broad current of the river flowed smoothly past, its surface now unbroken, no evidence that fish ever had been there at all. The jets still thundered overhead, their running lights now brilliant in the wet gloom. Traffic roared by on the freeway in a confusing blaze of light and noise. I rowed back toward the burned house.

I had hooked seven big salmon, and lost them all. There had been some moments of wild excitement, for which I was grateful, but there was still the disappointment of not having landed a single fish. But now, at least, I had the experience, the precedent on which to draw on future occasions. And I was confident that with the same fly on a larger hook, I would not fail the next time.

I spent the evening tying flies, and went back the next afternoon on the rising tide. But it had rained hard all through the night and most of the day, and the runoff from the farms and parking lots of the upper valley had brought the river up and muddied it with silt. The salmon were there again, rolling out in the current, but the water was so dirty they could not see my fly.

The rain went on for several days, and by the time the river had returned to normal flow the salmon run was over. Of course I tried again the next year, in the Duwamish and in other spots. But never again have I found the salmon in such a taking mood, never again have they come so willfully for my fly with all the strength born of the sea. Perhaps there was some subtle thing I did that day that escapes me now, something that means all the difference between failure and success. If so, I can't remember what it might have been. But I will always remember that afternoon of wild excitement in the rain, hooking great salmon while the sounds of the city echoed all around me. And one day, I know, the salmon will come again as they did then.

# A Lady
# Named Lenice

October morning.

The tires of the truck made a swishing sound on the pavement, still wet from the morning's rain. The peaks surrounding the mountain pass already were white with early snow. Winter had come early to the timberline country, but everywhere else fall still was in its glory.

The trip through the mountains to the Columbia Basin always is an interesting one, the country moving quickly past like a colored mural of changing shapes and images. In few other places can so much change be seen in so short a distance. There is the western slope with its thick fir forests drenched in rain, its old alders heavy with hanging moss; there is the mountain pass, its tangled peaks white with snow above the thick stands of alpine fir and spruce; and then there is the eastern slope, with the fir giving way quickly to the pine, and the golden aspens shaking themselves in the creek bottoms. The forest gives way to rolling hills of amber grass, and as the highway begins the last, long plunge to the Columbia River Gorge, the grass gives way to sage and dry coulees.

The Columbia is no longer a river where the highway crosses it; it is a vast, stillwater lake, its flow choked by the dam visible downstream from the windbattered bridge. From the bridge it is but a short drive south to the point where muddy Crab Creek flows out of its canyon and loses itself in the remnants of the river.

A decade ago, Crab Creek was a lonely, desolate place. The great winds that sweep up the Columbia River Gorge turn sharply into the canyon and blow along its length, whipping cyclones of sand and tumbleweeds before them. It was a dry, unfriendly place, frequented by jackrabbits, rattlesnakes and coyotes. A few isolated farms stood at its eastern end, and cattle roamed through the dead coulees, searching for sparse bunchgrass among the sage. The sluggish creek ran muddy in all seasons, with carp splashing in its shallows, and there was no reason for a trout fisherman to venture there.

But then the canyon changed. Upland farmers irrigated their lands with water from the river's reservoirs; the water flowed from the fields, seeking a way back to the river, seeping into the sandy soil. It surfaced again in the dry coulees at the bottom of the canyon, breaking through the soil in cool springs, flowing down the canyon wall in little streams. It filled a coulee and made a lake, spilled over its end and ran deeper into the canyon, forming a second lake. The second lake filled and again the water sought an outlet, flowing farther down, forming another lake and still another. And in the short space of a few years, the dead, dry canyon bottom was covered by the waters of four sparkling lakes.

The merciless rays of the summer sun reached into their depths and brought life out of them. Aquatic insects found a haven in the drowned sage, and enormous numbers of damselflies, dragonflies, chironomids and mayflies hatched in the lakes. Shrimp found their way into them and snails found the waters rich and hospitable. Rainbow trout were stocked and grew quickly to enormous size and weight on the great abundance of food.

The oldest lake, and the first to contain fish, was named Lenice, and it was Lenice where Enos Bradner and I were headed on this October day. We drove down the last stretch of gravel road to the cleared spot which was as far as vehicles could go. From there it was a quarter-mile trail through the desert rock and sand to the lakeshore.

Lenice is a large lake, and though it is possible to fish successfully from shore, it is easier to fish from a boat. The quarter-mile hike keeps many anglers from trying this, but others have rigged ingenious sets of wheels to carry their boats into the lake. Brad's boat already was there, his friends having carried it in earlier and left it padlocked to a fence post. I mounted my own boat on the set of wheels I had brought with me and we set out across the desert for the lake, invisible from the road.

Lenice is more than just an exciting place to fish. It also is the scene of a research program which, it is hoped, will lead to better fishing there and in many other waters.

When the lake was opened to fishing, the rich productivity of its waters was recognized by the Washington Game Department and it was restricted to "quality" fishing. Only artificial lures with barbless hooks were allowed; bait was outlawed and the limit was reduced to three fish a day over twelve inches. In the first two years, the rainbow trout in the lake grew quickly, some of them reaching weights of five pounds or more. With the great source of feed in the lake, they should have grown much larger, but few, if any, did. Instead, they reached sexual maturity at the age of two years or a little more, and most of them died.

To the anglers who fished the lake, this was no real surprise; they had come to expect it from their experiences in other lakes. The reason is that the rainbow trout now stocked by nearly all the Western states is far removed from the wild rainbow that was found by the first settlers. Population growth and the advent of "put-and-take" fishing that accompanied it led management officials to try to develop fast-breeding strains of rainbow trout so that new crops for stocking could be raised in as little time as possible. Those trout which matured at the earliest age were selected for brood stock in the hatcheries. The final, inevitable result was a strain of rainbow trout that spawned at the age of two years or even less.

This was a desirable goal from the standpoint of "put-and-take" management, where it makes good economic sense to have such fish. But these same fish were stocked in the "quality" lakes, where the intent of management was to produce fewer, larger fish. The trout grew rapidly in these lakes, but because of their genetic history they became sexually mature before they had lived long enough to grow to real trophy size. Few of them survived the effects of sexual maturation to grow larger.

Cognizant of this trend, the members of the Washington Fly Fishing Club proposed the Lenice Lake experiment. Financing the program themselves, and with the cooperation of the University of Washington Cooperative Fisheries Research Unit and the Department of Game, they proposed the following: Lenice Lake should be stocked each year with trout from the short-lived hatchery strain and an equal number of wild trout with a genetic history of longevity. Then, for a five-year period, the population would be monitored by creel censuses and netting and tagging operations to see which strain of fish lived longer and grew larger.

A search was made for a strain of wild trout, and finally eggs from the Kamloops trout in Pennask Lake, British Columbia, were obtained. These Kamloops trout spawn at an average age of four years, and this, according to the theory behind the experiment, would give them at least two years more growth than the hatchery fish.

The experiment now is in its third year, and the first plant of Kamloops trout is beginning to reach large size. Two years of work remain before any conclusions can be drawn, but in the meantime Lenice Lake has provided some of the most memorable fishing ever seen in the Northwest.

I rolled my boat down the last sandy grade to the lake-shore and Brad and I began to rig up for the fishing day ahead. I had been there only two weeks previously and had enjoyed one of the finest days in my memory. Anchored in the shallow west end of the lake, I had landed seven fish consecutively, each of them over four pounds, each of them desperately strong. All of them had run far into the backing, and each alone would have made my day on some other lake. An eighth fish of a size at least equal to all the rest had run my line around a submerged sagebrush plant and broken the leader. And so I had expectations of another wonderful day as we pushed our boats away from the shore and started rowing for the same place at the western end.

It was a typical fall day in the Columbia Basin. A solid, high overcast hid the sun and a changing breeze chased riffles across the water. The great hatches of spring were long gone, but a second generation of damselfly and dragonfly nymphs was active in the water. Coots clucked and bobbed in the shallows and the cattails were alive with the raucous calls of yellow-headed blackbirds. A marsh hawk glided on motionless wings over the swampy ground at the end of the lake.

We anchored our boats in the shallows and began to probe among the weeds and sunken brush with sinking flies. There was little surface activity, but occasionally we would be startled by the sound of a fierce, heavy rise from a large fish feeding. It became quickly obvious that there would be no fast fishing as there had been two weeks before; the trout were more cautious now, having been fished heavily since the opening of the fall season, and the algae bloom that had been on the lake earlier was gone, the water was clear, and no doubt the trout were more wary because of this.

Still, it was not long before I felt a hard, vicious strike, and a trout ran well with my fly, leaping high and tumbling at the end of its long run. It was a strong fish, and I coaxed the tackle to its limit to keep it from the thick weeds that grew within inches of the surface in many spots around. There was a satisfying feel to the plunging rod that signaled a heavy fish, and it fought stubbornly, showing itself in silver glimpses as it twisted and drove vainly to reach the bottom. Eventually it tired, and I led it to the net. I weighed it quickly in the net and it pulled the spring balance down nearly to the five-pound mark; a good start for the day, I thought. And as I twisted the fly free from its jaw, I saw where it had been hooked at least three times before. A good example of the quality concept: at least three anglers had enjoyed sport with this prime fish before I had; with luck, others would do so after I released it.

But after that the fishing was very slow for me. I caught and released a couple of scrappy smaller fish, but as the afternoon wore on nothing more moved to my fly.

Brad, meanwhile, had maneuvered his boat into a shallow pocket inshore of a small island, and there he found a school of large fish lying in among the weeds. He took three or four in rapid-fire order, setting quickly against the solid strikes, steering them masterfully through the weeds, bringing them to the net and releasing them. The old man was in his element, as excited as a boy, and I admired the enthusiasm that he could still feel after so many fish on so many waters in his long, illustrious life.

After that there was no action for either of us for a long while. The overcast grew darker with approaching twilight; soon it would be time to go, and I had taken only the one good fish.

The boat was drifting on a soft breeze that was pushing it gently toward the line of cattails that grew along the shore, where the coots still played noisily. I cast in front of the drifting craft, searching the water in a semicircle, hoping for one more good fish to end the day. And suddenly it was there, a hard strike followed by the sight of a big rainbow coming out in an arching leap, returning to the water with a heavy splash.

"Sounds like a big one," Brad's voice said across the water.

"It is," I said, and held on as the trout ran far along the edge of the cattails and jumped again. The wind quickened a little and began to push the boat faster toward the shore. There would be no chance to land the fish before the wind carried the boat into the cattails; somehow I had to stop its progress. Trying to keep the line taut with the rod in one hand, I worked an oar with the other, backing water, praying that the fish would not find a handy sagebrush plant and foul the leader. I gained a few feet and used both hands to play the fish, now slugging it out with shakes of its heavy head. Then the wind gained the upper hand again, and it was back to one hand on the rod and one hand on the oar until once again I had room to play the fish.

In that awkward way I fought the fish until its rushes grew shorter and it came obediently as I reeled in the last line until the leader knot was up to the tip-top of the rod. Then the wind was pushing on the boat again, carrying it toward the threatening line of cattails; quickly, I stabbed at the fish with the net. The mesh closed around it and I lifted it, dripping and squirming, from the lake. It was no longer than the big fish I had caught earlier, but it was immensely broad and thick. On the pocket scale it weighed more than five pounds, the largest trout I ever had taken in Lenice, and somehow it made the trip out easier as I wrestled the heavy boat up the sandy grade.

The fierce winds still blow up Crab Creek Canyon, and when they blow no trout fisherman goes there. It is still good country for jackrabbits, rattlesnakes and coyotes, and the cattle still graze on the dry hillsides. But now the chain of lakes at the bottom of the canyon is something of a mecca for Northwest anglers, and they come on the calm days to fish for the big rainbows that lurk among the sunken sage. The Kamloops trout are growing large and strong and hold the promise that in future years a five-pounder may no longer be unusual. Outwardly, the canyon still appears a foreboding place, but those anglers who are willing to challenge the heat and the barren, broken country will find Lenice a lake with rich rewards, and exciting promise for the future.

# The Track
## of a Trout

The boat seemed suspended over a black abyss populated with the ghosts of fishes moving quickly in thrusts of pale, milky light. The landmarks of the estuary had long since been lost in the approach of night, and now there was no other light at all except the far twinkle of lamps in a small town miles distant across the dark water. There was no sound except for the persistent, eerie echo that came to me through a pair of earphones from a sonic tag planted in the belly of a sea-run cutthroat trout.

It seems there ought to be a simple key to the behavior of the sea-run cutthroat, some single explanation that would lead to understanding of its habits and movements. But perhaps that is a forelorn hope. Anglers, being human, think more or less in logical patterns, and they seem to expect the same of fish. But there is no reason to believe that fish are capable of any sort of logic, and so the search to find some rational explanation for their movements probably is doomed in advance to failure. Yet fishermen still search, and perhaps it is the fun of searching that keeps them going.

It was as a part of this search that I found myself at Dewatto estuary on this dark, overcast night, listening to the pulse from a trout hidden from sight but not from sound.

Dewatto is a bay in Hood Canal, a deep cut carved by the Dewatto River which flows into it. The name is a corruption of the Indian word *Du-a-ta*, which meant "the place where sprites come out of the ground." On this evening it seemed an appropriate name as we watched the silent, phosphorescent wakes left by countless fish moving through the plankton of the estuary. It was easy to believe how these strange, glowing shapes in the sea had led the Indians to imagine ghosts emerging from the dark waters to stalk through the forests that grow down to the water's edge.

The chain of events that had taken us to Dewatto had begun months before in a conversation among cutthroat-fishing enthusiasts in the Washington Fly Fishing Club. Cutthroat traditionally are caught on the rising tide, and few anglers can recall having seen them at low water. The question, debated for years, was where do the cutthroat go during low water, and why?

The members decided to pool their money to buy some sonic tags and track the movements of cutthroat. The money was quickly raised and more than thirty members volunteered to take part in the experiment. Battery-powered tags were purchased, one emitting a fast-pulsed sound signal and the other a slower pulse. Tracking gear was borrowed from a government agency, and on the appointed weekend the club members flocked to Dewatto with campers, trailers and boats to begin the experiment.

Dewatto had been chosen because it is well sheltered from the southwesters which regularly sweep the open waters of the canal, and because it was a place where anglers had taken cutthroat regularly on the fly. The plan was to use a beach seine to capture fish on Friday evening, then plant the sonic tags in the two largest fish and track them around the clock through Monday. But at first the beach seines yielded nothing, and it was Saturday morning before a club member succeeded in taking a cutthroat on the fly. The fish was partly anesthetized and the capsule-shaped tag worked down its gullet and into its stomach before it was returned to the estuary.

Later in the day, the seine finally turned up a second fish, a husky nineteen-incher, and the second tag was planted. And then the club members began following the movements of the fish, using boats to trail the telltale echoes and plotting the positions of the trout on charts of the estuary.

It was nearly dark on Sunday when I arrived for my "shift." Most of the members had gone home by then and the few of us remaining gathered in a camper to draw up a schedule for the night. At ten o'clock I climbed into a boat with Curt Jacobs and he took the oars to steer us gingerly out into the dark estuary. Each stroke of the oars set the water afire with pale, shifting waves of phosphorescent light, with bright, gleaming sparks here and there among them.

As we moved past a row of old pilings to the deeper water of the estuary, we began to see the tracks of countless small fish, glowing with ghostly flame as they darted away. Occasionally, a larger fish—perhaps a salmon—would swim by, and we could measure its length in light. Curt struck his foot against the side of the aluminum boat and the water exploded with light as a thousand fish fled the sound like Roman candles in the fog.

I donned the earphones and checked the listening gear, which consisted of a cone-shaped hydrophone mounted on a metal shaft, with wires leading to an amplifier and then to the earphones. By dipping the hydrophone in the water and turning it until the sound signal reached its peak it was possible to take a bearing on the direction of the sound. Then the boat would be moved to another location to take another bearing so that a fix on the fish could be obtained by triangulation and noted on the chart.

I thrust the hydrophone over the side and soon picked up the faint, chirping signal from one of the fish. We followed the sound, using flashlights to spot landmarks on the shore to plot our position, and got a fix on the trout in shallow water near the mouth of the river. Then Curt started the motor on the stern and we moved to the mouth of the estuary where the other fish had last been pinpointed, leaving a trail of phosphorescent fire in our wake.

A faint breeze stirred the water at the estuary's mouth and tiny wavelets slapped against the sides of the boat. Occasionally, out in the darkness, we could hear the heavy splash of a leaping salmon. We quickly picked up the signal from the second fish and plotted its position, which had changed little from the last plot.

I looked at my wristwatch and was surprised to find that an hour had passed. Curt started the motor again and we headed back toward the camp, with Curt steering and I in the bow with a flashlight to search for pilings and deadheads in our path. Back at camp, Curt headed for a sleeping bag in the back of his truck and I roused Harry Ludwig from his. For the next hour Harry and I tracked the fish, which had moved little, and then I turned in for a few hours' sleep while Harry woke Dick Thompson to continue tracking.

At five o'clock I got up to join Harry for another tracking session. The tide had run far out, and with our flashlights and lanterns we could see that most of the estuary was bare mudflat with little more than the river running through it. As we shined our lights across the river to the far bank, two pairs of glowing eyes stared back at us—perhaps raccoons, or even bears, that had come down from the woods.

The lower water made it difficult to maneuver the boat, and the last watch had lost track of both fish. This was the crucial test: to find where the cutthroat had gone at extreme low water. So far we had no idea where they were.

Harry and I made our way out through the sticky mud to the small, water-filled channel where the last tracking crew had left the boat. We pushed off into the shallow water, less than three feet deep and clogged with heavy mats of eelgrass. There was nowhere to go but downstream; upstream it was too shallow for the boat.

"I've got a hunch," I told Harry. "Before we go anywhere, let's take a sounding right here." We dipped the hydrophone into the shallow water and the grass, and immediately there came a strong signal. With a little maneuvering we determined that one of the cutthroat was almost directly beneath the boat, holding in the protection of the thick grass.

Having noted the fish's position on the chart, we slowly worked our way downstream, shining lights over the side to keep from running aground on the mudbanks. As we got closer to the mouth of the estuary, the water deepened and the flashlights caught patches of gravel showing through the mud, and soon we were in the open water of the canal. Using the motor, we cruised back and forth until we picked up a signal from the second fish and found it holding close to shore off the north headland at the estuary's mouth.

We plotted the position of the fish and then drifted, talking and drinking coffee from our vacuum bottles, watching the phosphorescent display. After a while we took a second sounding and found that the fish now was on the move. The tide was changing, imperceptibly to us but not to the trout, and we followed the fish as it began to move rapidly into the estuary toward the mouth of the stream. For perhaps a quarter of a mile we followed and then took a final fix of its position as it became time for us to wake up the next watch.

I crawled back in my sleeping bag and slept until after it was light, then fixed a breakfast and rejoined the tracking effort. The tide was high now, but the relative positions of the two fish had not changed much. One was resting under a log close to shore, well up in the estuary and not far from the channel where we had found it at low water. The other trout still was at the mouth of the estuary, moving occasionally, but not far.

We combined fishing with tracking through the day, casting in the likely spots and breaking every half hour or so to plot the positions of the tagged fish. Through the morning and afternoon they hardly moved. I took two trout on the fly, one with a stomach full of sticklebacks and the other filled with fir needles, maple seeds and bits of leaf, indicating it had spent some time in fresh water upstream.

Both fish were bright-silver, typical of cutthroat in salt water, and both were covered with sea lice, copepods that attach themselves to the backs and bellies of trout.

At four o'clock I quit fishing to make a final plot on the two fish. The first still was content under its log, but the second had moved, and at first I could not pick up its signal. Steering the boat back and forth across the mouth of the estuary, I finally picked up a faint signal and followed it until I found the fish, a mile out in deep water and still moving. After that, we packed our gear and set out for home.

And so the experiment was at an end, and it was time to evaluate what we had learned. Somewhat to our disappointment, but not necessarily to our surprise, the plots revealed little discernible pattern to the movements of the trout other than a general tendency to swim in with the flood tide and out with the ebb. And so our search for some common denominator to the behavior of the nomadic cutthroat was, in this case at least, largely unsuccessful.

Still, it is difficult to draw hard conclusions from such an experiment. Three days, perhaps, was too short a time to track the fish. A longer time might have revealed a more meaningful pattern to their movements. Perhaps at a different time of year or in a different place the trout would have behaved differently. And who is to say that their behavior at Dewatto was natural with the strange burden of the sonic tags in their bellies?

So we know little more than we knew before, and what little we have learned offers no encouragement to anglers who seek the cutthroat in salt water. Yet it seems safe to say that as long as cutthroat continue to prowl the beaches, anglers will continue to search for them there, relying on luck and persistence if not knowledge.

# The End
# of the Year

And so the cycle now is nearly at its end. The earth once more has completed its whirling course, and its life has followed the well-ordered sequence of the seasons, the rise and fall of the tide, the rising and setting of the sun.

Always there is a little sorrow at the passing of the year, perhaps because each of us realizes another year is gone and our time on earth is measured less. But the feeling passes quickly, supplanted by the return of the old fever, the familiar excitement of the chase. Always, it seems, there is time for at least one more trip before the snow flies, before the rivers run with the first winter floods.

Sometimes the last fish of a year is as memorable as the first, memorable in size or strength or circumstance. One year on the trout season's last day the termites hatched in the forest and the wind swept them out on the lake in countless numbers where they fell and struggled on the surface, and the trout fed on them wildly. I had nothing to imitate them, but in the bottom of a fly box I found a large Green Drake tied with hackle-point wings. I spread the wings flat and coated the body with mucilin paste to hide its color, then cast the unlikely fly to the feeding trout. In their unwary anxiety to feed, three of them took it, and one was a strong, fat rainbow, one of the best of the year.

Another year there was ice around the edge of Morgan Lake on the day before Thanksgiving, but the rainbows still were active and feeding. They came willingly to the fly, fighting well, each of them a near twin to all the others, all of them weighing within ounces of two pounds. The next strike was no different in feel from all the others, but by the time I raised the rod the backing splice already had run out through the guides and an enormous trout was jumping far across the lake. It jumped free and escaped before I had a clear look at it, but there was little doubt it had been the largest trout of the season.

Disappointed, I fished on into the cold gloom of the evening, and then another great trout took my fly. In the gathering darkness I played it to the net, a great old buck, and I decided it was a good fish to end the year.

Even in December when the Basin lakes freeze over and the rivers flood, the sea-run cutthroat still move in and out on the tide and there is no lack of fishing. Braving the winter gusts and the stinging sleet, hardy anglers fish on through the short, dark days that signal the dying of the year. In every month, in every season, there are men who fish as long as there are trout or salmon in the rivers and the bays.

Why do men fish? What is it that makes angling not just

a sport, but a philosophy and a way of life? Many good men have addressed themselves to that question throughout the long literature of angling. Their answers vary; some contend it is instinct inherited from man's early days as a hunter and gatherer, and some say it is because fish are found in such pleasant places; some say they fish because fishing is a contemplative sport, and some because it is a gentle art that relieves them from the pressures of their daily lives.

I suspect it is a little of all of these things, and something more. I suspect each individual angler has his individual reason, whether or not it is within his power to express it, even to himself. Indeed, it is difficult for me to know my own reasons; but I think I fish because there is a challenge in it, and because fishing forces the angler to observe nature and become a part of it. I fish because I love rivers and the life in them, because I love their sound and color and quick move-ment and the scent of forests on their shores. I fish because trout and salmon are honest and uncompromising creatures and one can meet them only on their terms.

I fish because fishing takes me to places where the land is still as it always has been, and as long as such places still exist there is hope for mankind. I fish because fishing humbles a man, and humility is a rare virtue. But most of all, I fish because it makes me feel closer to myself.

For whatever reason men fish, they are rewarded simply by the things they see. All the mechanisms of life are visible to those who look for them, from the nature of the very smallest creatures to the natures of men. A man's behavior on the stream is likely to tell much about the kind of man he is, and the deepest friendships are those made along rivers. And perhaps this is another good reason why men fish.

In his searching, the angler sees many things. Often he is the first to notice change, because change always has meaning for an angler. It may be nothing more than the subtle shifting of the current in a river, a day's delay in a faithful hatch, or

some small thing a casual observer would not see or understand. But often the change is sweeping and drastic; a forest
cut away to change forever a river's flow; a dam; a bridge; a
new road where there was none before.

In this book, I have written often of change. And the
changes that have come to the watersheds, the forests, the
rivers and the wilderness seldom are for the good. Always they
are justifiable in terms of profit, economics or convenience,
but rarely are they good for the land, the creatures that live on
it or the waters that flow through it.

The technology of man has given him almost infinite
power to destroy life, but little knowledge to restore it. Early
in our history the land was so vast and so wild it seemed there
never would be an end to it, nor to the fish and game that it
sustained. Now the end clearly is in sight, but the human
juggernaut rolls on, unchecked. Though now it is possible for
man to enjoy a life of plenty without the total, wasteful
destruction of resources, the momentum of the past still
carries forward the bulldozers and the dams.

There must be a better way, and all who love nature
share a responsibility to help in finding it. There is more at
stake than the future of angling; the future of man also rests in
the balance, and time is running out. The Year of the Angler
is coming to a close, and it is time to think hard about the
future.

The year ebbs. It is raining now, and soon the rain will
become snow. In the high country the snow already is falling.
The maples and alders, once bright, are starkly barren now,
their dark, decaying leaves tumbling in the currents of the
rivers flowing down from the hills. The rivers are running slow
and dark, but the salmon still are there. Like the leaves, they
have lost their brightness, and the once great silver shapes are
ugly now, black and yellow with fungus, fins worn ragged by
their spawning ordeal. Their last life ebbs along with the last

moments of the year. Another cycle nears its end, another ring is added to the tree.

Some who were with us when the year began are not with us now; for them there are memories of shared campfires, of laughter and disappointment, of days both difficult and fruitful. Their cycle, too, is ended, but we will keep their memories with us as we continue on our own.

The earth is hushed, waiting the ordeal of winter. The farms and the fields are barren and bleak, and there is ice on the rims of the marshes. The ducks and geese are long departed for the warmer south, and the bright songs of the summer birds are still.

A cold, wet mist floats thickly in the forests, and the old cedars and the firs loom through it like gray ghosts from another time. There is only the slow, even drip of rain and the silence of decay as rotting limbs and dead leaves return forever to the soil.

As the year came softly in the January dawn, so it softly goes in the late December dusk. The sky is dark and low, and the first snowflakes begin to fall in aimless, twisting patterns, growing ever thicker until they form a solid moving wall of white. The snow collects in the crevices between the rocks on the river bars, fills them and grows deeper. It clings like fragile lace to the fir limbs and gathers in the crotches of the naked alders. It hides the wounds of clear-cuts on the foothill slopes and masks the filth of the city streets. It swirls through the distant valleys and mingles with the woodsmoke from the cabin chimneys, falls gently on the meadows and holds the fresh, bold track of a foraging deer.

It has been a good year, and it dies peacefully and well. But there is no end to time or life; life sleeps, and awaits the beginning of another year.